Trivial Pursuit ™

Sport

THE AUTHORIZED GAME BOOK

GUINNESS BOOKS

Design: Clive Sutherland
Design concept and cover design: Craig Dodd

Printed in Great Britain by The Bath Press Ltd, Avon

'Guinness' is a registered trade mark of Guinness Superlatives Ltd

Trivial Pursuit is a game and trademark owned and licensed by Horn
Abbot International Limited

**British Library Cataloguing in Publication Data**
Trivial Pursuit : pocket edition : sport.
  1. Sports — Miscellanea
  796'.076      GV706.8

  ISBN 0-85112-875-0

HORN ABBOT
INTERNATIONAL

New from Guinness — **The Pocket Edition of Trivial Pursuit!** The slimline Pocket Edition has been specially designed so that trivia fans can carry with them more than 1000 tantalizing trivia questions wherever they go. Now you can play Trivial Pursuit in the car, waiting for a bus, on a train, even in the bath — you need never be bored again.

Each Pocket Edition is arranged in quizzes, with the answers at the back of the book for easy reference. And to make sure that there's something for everyone there are three other separate titles — **Genus, Rock and Pop,** and **The Movies,** each containing hours of classic trivia challenge!

## SPORT EDITION

This Sport Pocket Edition contains 54 quizzes divided into six categories. The categories are coded:

| | |
|---|---|
| (C) | Champions |
| (BS) | Ball Sports |
| (OG) | Olympic Games |
| (RS) | Race Sports |
| (FE) | Famous Events |
| (W) | Who? What? Where? When? |

**1** Who was the first British champion to win three Lonsdale belts outright?

**2** Who took Randolph Turpin's world middleweight title from him?

**3** Who defended the world heavyweight title most times?

**4** From whom did Cassius Clay win the heavyweight title?

**5** Who was the only English-born heavyweight champion of the world?

**6** Who defeated Don Curry to become world welterweight champion in 1986?

**7** Who was the last bare-knuckle heavyweight champion?

**8** Who took part in the 'thrilla in Manila' in 1975?

**9** Which two brothers have held versions of the world heavyweight title?

**10** Which two boxers in 1921 drew the first million-dollar gate?

**11** What does 'Barry' stand for in Barry McGuigan's name?

**12** Who knocked out Pat Cowdell in the first round of a world featherweight title fight in 1985?

**13** Who was the unsuccessful challenger in three consecutive heavyweight title fights in 1947, 1948 and 1949?

**14** Who is the only world champion to be born in Antigua?

**15** Who beat Sugar Ray Robinson when he challenged for the world light-heavyweight title?

**16** Which world heavyweight champion fought most often as a professional?

**17** Before Marvin Hagler, who was the last boxer to be world middleweight champion for more than five years?

**18** Who is the only man to win the world heavyweight title on a foul?

**19** Who was killed in a plane crash when flying to fight Jake LaMotta for the world middleweight title?

**20** In this picture Barry McGuigan wins the world featherweight championship, but who is the former champion on his way to the canvas?

**1** This man is the joint leading scorer in internationals for Wales — who is he?

**2** Which club celebrated its centenary on Christmas Day 1986?

**3** Blackpool play in what colour shirts?

**4** For which club did the England half-back line of Britton, Cullis, Mercer play during the Second World War?

**5** Who managed Arsenal when they performed the League Championship and FA Cup double?

**6** Why was the 1970 FA Cup Final unique in Wembley history?

7) Which club was the first to win three consecutive Football League Championships?

8) Which club was the last to win three consecutive Football League Championships?

9) Which club achieved a bye in the 1986–7 Littlewoods Cup because Luton refused to allow their supporters to watch?

10) Who were the English and Welsh strikers who joined Barcelona for the 1986–7 season?

11) Who was England's manager before Alf Ramsey?

12) Which League club plays at The Shay?

13) Real Madrid won the first five European Cups — who won the sixth?

14) Which English player was European Footballer of the Year twice in succession?

15) Who accepted Liverpool's Milk Cup at Wembley in 1983?

16) Who was the 'Galloping Major' who helped humiliate England in 1953?

17) Dixie Dean's record 60 League goals in 1927–8 beat the previous best total of 59 by which player?

18) Whom did Celtic beat in the final when they won the European Cup?

19) Who kept goal for 1142 minutes in international matches without conceding a goal?

20) Which two teams shared the first nine Scottish Cups?

**1** Who won the men's 800 metres in the 1980 Moscow Olympics?

**2** Who won the men's 800 metres in the 1984 Los Angeles Olympics?

**3** How many hurdles are there in the 400 metres hurdles?

**4** Which British male won the 400 metres hurdles gold medal in 1968?

**5** Why was American Frank Shorter's marathon victory in Munich pleasing and appropriate?

**6** Who won the women's 100 metres sprint in 1984?

**7** Who was the New Zealand runner who won the 1500 metres in 1936?

**8** What did multiple gold medal winner Paavo Nurmi carry in his hand in many of his races?

**9** Which women's race was first run in 1928 but not again until 1960 because it was considered too exhausting?

**10** Who were the two gold medalists whose stories were told in the film *Chariots of Fire*?

**11** In which event was Guy Drut the first non-English speaking athlete to win the gold medal?

**12** Who deprived Wendy Sly of a gold medal in the 1984 Olympics by beating her into second place?

**13** Who was the Italian sprinter who made the 200 metres final four times from 1972 to 1984, winning it once?

**14** How did Jesse Owens come to be called 'Jesse', which was not his name?

**15** Which British athlete won a gold medal in 1964 and married the men's team captain?

**16** What mistake was made in the 1932 steeplechase at Los Angeles?

**17** The three medallists in the 1972 5000 metres are pictured already in the lead — who are they?

**18** Who was the British gold medal winner in 1956 who was disqualified, and reinstated three hours later?

**19** What was Roger Bannister's best placing in an Olympic event?

**20** What happened to Frank Baumgartl in the 1976 steeplechase?

**1** On which racecourse is the Derby run?

**2** Which Derby winner was kidnapped in 1983?

**3** Who, between 1930 and 1948, owned a 20th-century record five Derby winners?

**4** Which horse provided Lester Piggott with his first Derby winner?

**5** Which six-times winning jockey was encouraged by the cries of 'Come on, Steve'?

**6** This picture shows the finish of the 1977 Derby, with Lester Piggott scoring his eighth victory. Can you name two of the first three to finish?

**7** Why might some runners in the Derby carry a different weight to others?

8. Why was the 1984 winner *Running Rein* disqualified?

9. Which horse was Sir Gordon Richards' only Derby winner?

10. Which horse holds the record time for the Derby?

11. How many Derby winners did Lester Piggott ride?

12. Which future Prix de l'Arc de Triomphe winner did *Roberto* beat by a short head in 1972?

13. Why is the 1913 Derby associated with the Suffragette movement?

14. On which horse did Steve Cauthen win the Derby in 1985?

15. What did the winners *Jeddah*, *Signorinetta* and *Aboyeur* have in common?

16. When was the Derby first run — a) 1700  b) 1780 or c) 1870?

17. Who tossed a coin with Lord Derby for the privilege of lending his name to the race?

18. Which was the last Derby winner ridden by Charlie Smirke?

19. Who was the man who loved, owned and trained the winners *Blakeney* (1969) and *Morston* (1973)?

20. What did *Pinza* (1953), *Crepello* (1957), *Hard Ridden* (1958) and *St Paddy* (1960) have in common?

**1** Who captained Tottenham Hotspur to the Football League and FA Cup double?

**2** Which Second Division side defeated Leeds United in the 1973 FA Cup Final?

**3** Who scored for both sides in the 1946 Derby County v. Charlton Athletic FA Cup Final?

**4** Who scored the winning goal in the 'Matthews Final' in 1953?

**5** Which team lost in the first Wembley Cup Final?

**6** Who scored the first goal in the 1986 FA Cup Final?

**7** Goalkeeper Dick Pym, who kept a clean sheet in three Cup Finals — 1923, 1926 and 1929 — played for which side?

**8** Who played for West Ham in the 1964 Final, and against them in 1975 — was it a) Bobby Moore b) Geoff Hurst or c) Martin Peters?

**9** Which club has won the FA Cup seven times in seven finals?

**10** For whom did Mike Trebilcock score two goals, helping his team to win after being two down?

**11** Who scored the only two goals in the 1981 Final, but still did not gain a winners' medal?

**12** Discounting replays, which is the only team to score three goals in the Final and lose?

**13** Which team was in three Finals in the 1960s and lost them all?

**14** Which was the last team to play in the FA Cup Final and be relegated in the same year?

**15** Who scored the winning goal for Arsenal in the FA Cup Final of 1971?

**16** Who won the Cup five times in its first seven years?

**17** Who won a winners' medal in the 1978 Final, was transferred to the losing team, and helped them win the following year?

**18** Photographed is the 1978 FA Cup Final. Who are the two Arsenal players, and in how many FA Cup Finals did they each appear?

**19** Who played in nine FA Cup Finals, winning five winners' medals?

**20** How many players played in all three of Everton's Cup Final sides in 1984, 1985 and 1986?

**1** Who is the only Briton to win an Olympic javelin gold medal?

**2** Who was the world boxing champion whose father sang in the Eurovision Song Contest?

**3** Who was the first jockey to be knighted?

**4** Who scored the only goal of the 1985 FA Cup Final?

**5** Who is the American who became champion jockey in Britain in the 1980s?

**6** Who was the first to be voted BBC TV 'Sports Personality of the Year' twice?

**7** Who scored 1000 runs and took 100 wickets in the 1984 cricket season?

**8** Who was the world boxing champion whose sister took over from Diana Ross in the Supremes pop group?

**9** Who has scored most League goals for Everton?

**10** Who rode the winner of the Grand National in the film *National Velvet*?

**11** Who captained the Rest of the World side in England in 1970, when the South African cricket tour was cancelled?

**12** Who rode his first Classic winner on *Tap on Wood* in 1979?

**13** Who refereed the second Ali v. Liston world title fight?

**14** Who was the first player to score 8000 runs in Test cricket?

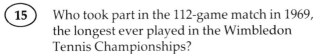

**(15)** Who took part in the 112-game match in 1969, the longest ever played in the Wimbledon Tennis Championships?

**(16)** Stirling Moss was one of two British drivers who each won two grand prix motor races in 1956 — who was the other?

**(17)** Who beat Fatima Whitbread with the last javelin throw of the 1983 world athletics championships?

**(18)** Which famous singer bought triple world champion Henry Armstrong's contract?

**(19)** Who won the hammer gold medal for England at three successive Commonwealth games, 1962 to 1970?

**(20)** Who is this Scot who won the award for the most stylish boxer of the 1956 Olympic Games?

**1** Which British television commentator was born in Berlin, and whose father, like himself, was a Ryder Cup golfer?

**2** Who is the only Japanese player to win the World Match-Play Championship?

**3** What is the distinction shared by Open Champions Arnauld Massy and Seve Ballesteros?

**4** Before Sandy Lyle and Tony Jacklin, who was the last Briton to win the Open Championship?

**5** Who beat Jack Nicklaus in the semi-final of the 1986 World Matchplay Championship?

**6** Who was the South African who won the Open Championship four times from 1949 to 1957?

**7** In 1986 this golfer became the third from his country to win the Open. Name all three.

**8** Who is the Australian golfer whose brother was a Test match wicket-keeper?

**9** Who won the Grand Slam of British and American Open and Amateur championships in 1930?

**10** What was odd about Bernhard Langer's victory in the 1981 German Open?

**11** Who, in 1970, held the British and US Open Championships simultaneously?

**12** Who recovered from a serious motor accident to win several major titles and became the subject of a film, *Follow the Sun*?

**13** Who was the first golfer to win the US Masters twice in succession?

**14** Who was the British golfer who won the French Open in 1973 and 1974?

**15** Who, in 1981, became the first Australian to win the US Open?

**16** Who captained the British team which won the Ryder Cup in 1957?

**17** Who is the only Argentinian to win the Open Championship?

**18** Which American golfer was an outstanding college footballer and won the US Open in 1974 wearing spectacles?

**19** Who won the 1979 US Masters after a play-off with Ed Snead and Tom Watson?

**20** Who was the first American-based golfer to win the Open Championship?

**1** What do the initials M.C.C. stand for?

**2** What is England's highest Test score against Australia?

**3** Which county won the NatWest trophy in 1986?

**4** The players who headed the English batting and bowling averages in 1986 played for which county?

**5** What were W. G. Grace's Christian names?

**6** In which town is the Woolloongabba Test match ground?

**7** Who was the 19-year-old Indian who in his second Test in 1984–5 took 12 England wickets?

**8** Which county has a ground from which can be seen a famous crooked church spire?

**9** What do LEG, TG and APE have in common?

**10** What is the surname of the seven brothers, all of whom played for Worcestershire?

**11** For which countries did Herbert Sutcliffe and Bert Sutcliffe play?

**12** Who played in a Sunday benefit match during his 79th Test for England and was never picked again?

**13** How many centuries did Denis Compton score in 1947?

**14** Who bowled Don Bradman first ball in a Test match?

**15** This man currently has taken most Test wickets. Who is he and whose record did he overtake?

**16** What is the first-class competition in which the West Indian islands play?

**17** Which P. G. Wodehouse character was named after a cricketer?

**18** Which American town sent teams to tour England, playing the counties in first-class matches?

**19** Which countries have played in tied Test matches?

**20** Why was Graham Gooch's Test debut unique among post-war English batsmen?

1. Which is this Olympic team at the opening ceremony of the Moscow Games and why is the lone representative carrying the Olympic flag?

2. Who founded the modern Olympic Games?

3. What do the five Olympic rings represent?

4. Who officially opened the 1956 Olympic Games?

5. Where were the first modern Olympic Games held?

6. What first was achieved by the athlete who lit the flame in the Mexico City Stadium in 1968?

**7** ) At the opening ceremony, which country's team is the first to enter the stadium?

**8** ) And which country's team is the last to enter the stadium?

**9** ) Which famous snooker player carried the Olympic torch in 1956?

**10** ) The first Olympic village was in Los Angeles — in which year?

**11** ) Who took the oath for the athletes at the 1984 Olympic Games in Los Angeles?

**12** ) When is the first mention of the Ancient Olympic Games — 776BC, 444BC, 216BC or 393AD?

**13** ) The first Olympic Games to be televised, on a closed-circuit system, was in which year?

**14** ) Who devised the opening ceremony for the 1960 Winter Olympic Games at Squaw Valley?

**15** ) Who succeeded Avery Brundage as the International Olympic Committee president?

**16** ) To whom is the Val Barker Trophy awarded at the Olympics?

**17** ) What does the athlete taking the Olympic oath hold?

**18** ) What does the Olympic motto, *Citius, Altius, Fortius* mean?

**19** ) What are the colours of the five Olympic rings?

**20** ) Where is the heart of Baron Pierre de Coubertin buried?

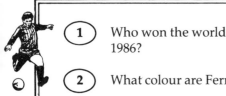

**1** Who won the world drivers' championship in 1986?

**2** What colour are Ferrari Formula 1 cars?

**3** Which driver has won the most grand prix?

**4** What nationality was five-times world champion Juan Fangio?

**5** How many times was Stirling Moss world champion?

**6** In which race did an accident kill 79 people in 1955?

**7** Which British race track opened in 1907, included a bridge over a river, and closed in 1939, being converted for aircraft manufacture?

**8** Which Australian driver drove a car manufactured by himself to the world drivers' championship in 1966?

**9** Which peer began a Formula 1 team and engaged James Hunt as driver?

**10** Which Formula 1 racing car had six wheels?

**11** Which race includes in its winners Al Unser, A.J. Foyt, Jim Clark and Graham Hill?

**12** Who was the first Englishman to win the Formula 1 drivers' championship?

**13** Which make of British car won the Le Mans race five times between 1924 and 1930?

**14** Who was the posthumous winner of the world drivers' championship in 1970?

**15** Who was the first driver from the United States to win the world drivers' championship?

**16** How did Lella Lombardi make history in 1975?

**17** Which grand prix driver won six successive races in the 1952 season?

**18** Here is James Hunt, seen after his victory at the British Grand Prix at Brands Hatch in 1976. What was odd about this celebration?

**19** On which British track, part of the estate of the Duke of Richmond and Gordon, did Bruce McLaren suffer his fatal accident?

**20** Which British driver won the RAC Rally in 1976?

**1** Who was the first man to beat Muhammad Ali as a professional?

**2** Who was the first winner of the BBC's *Pot Black* competition?

**3** Which British soccer team was the first to win the European Cup?

**4** Who was the first to score a maximum break in the world snooker championships?

**5** Who are these cricketers, and what record was set by the one on the left at Headingley in 1977, and by the man on the right at Bombay in 1980?

**6** Who was the first heavyweight boxing champion to regain the title?

**7** Who was the first woman to win an Olympic marathon gold medal?

**8** Which team was the first to win the Football League Cup?

**9** Who, in 1983, was the first New Zealander to reach the Wimbledon men's singles final for 69 years?

**10** Who was Britain's first black boxing champion?

**11** Who was the first man to win the world speedway championship three years in succession?

**12** In which year was the FA Cup Final first televised in colour?

**13** Who was the first batsman to score a century in a Test match?

**14** Who won the first international soccer match?

**15** What unwanted first did Ewa Klobukowska achieve in athletics?

**16** Who was the first English player to be European Footballer of the Year — a) Billy Wright b) Stanley Matthews or c) Bobby Charlton?

**17** What first did Gertrude Ederle achieve in 1926?

**18** What first did M.P. Betts achieve under the pseudonym A.H. Chequer?

**19** Who won the first Open Golf Championship?

**20** Who, in 1973, was the first Soviet player to reach a Wimbledon singles final?

**1** What is kept in a small urn at Lord's cricket ground?

**2** What is the value of potting the red ball in billiards?

**3** What is known as 'Annie's room' at darts?

**4** What is the unit of measurement for the height of a horse?

**5** What is the show jumping competition which tests jumping ability over a limited number of large obstacles?

**6** What does ringing the bell in a track race signify?

**7** What was the name of the horse on which Princess Anne won the 1971 European three-day event championship?

**8** What is the second largest total on which it is possible to finish at darts?

**9** What sporting innovation was John Sholto Douglas responsible for under another name?

**10** What name is given to a left-hander's googly in cricket?

**11** What is the long jump called in the United States?

**12** What is a golfer's bogey?

**13** What number is at 'three o'clock' on a dartboard?

**14** What game are you playing if you are holding a yarborough?

**15** What do the New York Knickerbockers play?

**16** What do the initials RORC stand for?

**17** This is C.B. Fry batting in 1921. What country seriously considered making him king?

**18** What is black, 3 inches in diameter, 1 inch high, usually of vulcanised rubber, and cold?

**19** What are the New, the Eden and the Jubilee?

**20** What, in curling, if not well-soled, might develop a kiggle-caggle?

(1) Who is this man, the last player to beat Rod Laver in a Wimbledon final?

(2) Who holds the post-First World War record of five consecutive men's singles championships at Wimbledon?

(3) What was Billie-Jean King's maiden name under which she won her first Wimbledon title?

(4) Who were the brother and sister who won the Wimbledon mixed doubles in 1981?

(5) In which country was John McEnroe born?

(6) Which regular doubles partner of Billie-Jean King was related to a famous cellist?

(7) Who was beaten by Stan Smith in the 1972 men's singles final at Wimbledon?

(8) Who won the women's singles title at the US Open in 1985?

**9** Who is the only woman to have won every championship — singles, doubles and mixed doubles — at every Grand Slam tournament?

**10** Which two players did Boris Becker beat in the 1985 and 1986 Wimbledon singles finals?

**11** Which champion became Mrs Cawley?

**12** Who is the player, now British, who was born a Czech, but won the Wimbledon men's singles as an Egyptian?

**13** Who was beaten by Arthur Ashe in the Wimbledon men's singles final?

**14** Who won the last all-English singles final at Wimbledon?

**15** Who beat Mrs Lloyd and Miss Navratilova in separate finals of the US Open singles championship?

**16** How many times did Bjorn Borg win the US Open title?

**17** Who was Spain's finest player, the winner of the Wimbledon men's singles title in 1966?

**18** Who was the first man to win the Grand Slam of Wimbledon, Australian, French and US singles titles — a) Fred Perry  b) Rod Laver or c) Donald Budge?

**19** Who was the British player who won Wimbledon after being five times losing finalist in the world table tennis championship?

**20** Who was the first black player to win a Wimbledon singles championship?

1. What might a cricket umpire decide to do without if it is windy?

2. How high from the ground is the net in netball?

3. In soccer, how far is the penalty spot from the goal line?

4. What is the value of the brown ball in snooker?

5. How many clubs may a professional golfer use in a round?

6. Which game has 18 players each side, and is played on an oval pitch with goals which have centre and outer posts?

7. What is the minimum penalty score in snooker?

8. In American football, how long has the offensive team to put the ball in play after the referee's whistle signals the ball is ready?

9. How high is the net in tennis, at the centre?

10. In flat green bowls, how far from the mat must the jack travel before its delivery is valid?

11. In cricket, if the batsman strikes the ball and it hits a helmet discarded by a fielder, what is the umpire's decision?

12. What are the two broken lines down the centre of an American football field from goal line to goal line called?

13. In which sport is each goal inside an 18ft diameter circle called a goal crease?

14. What are the dimensions of the goal in soccer?

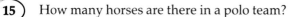

**15** How many horses are there in a polo team?

**16** How many players are there in a water polo team?

**17** What is 21 feet from the net on a tennis court?

**18** Michael Holding is bowling at the 1976 Oval Test in the photograph — but who is the umpire, a man who scored over 3000 runs in 1961?

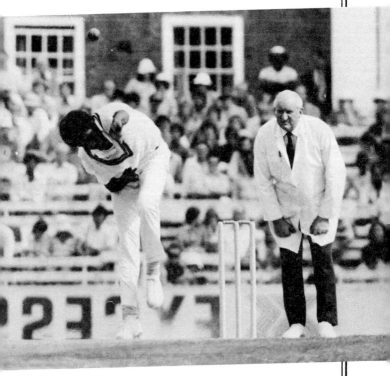

**19** In which game, played in a three-wall court, is the ball hit with a wicker basket called a *cesta*?

**20** Which form of football has a goal 21ft wide, with uprights 16ft high joined by a crossbar 8ft from the ground?

**1** In 1984 which athlete duplicated Jesse Owens' four gold medals of 1936?

**2** Who won the Olympic heavyweight boxing gold medal three times in succession?

**3** Who twice performed the double of 3000 metres and 10 000 metres at the same Olympics?

**4** Who is the only athlete to win two gold medals at 1500 metres?

**5** In which events did Valerie Brisco-Hookes win her three gold medals in 1984?

**6** Which country won the hockey Olympic gold medal six times running?

**7** What is the most gold medals won by one person at one Olympic Games, and who won them?

**8** How many Olympic decathalons has this man won — and how many times has he scored the most points in a single event within an Olympic decathalon?

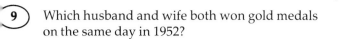

**9** Which husband and wife both won gold medals on the same day in 1952?

**10** Who won four gold medals at the same event in track and field?

**11** Who is the only sprinter, man or woman, to win the Olympic 100 metres twice (not counting the irregular 1906 Games)?

**12** Who was the Polish sprinter and long jumper who won seven gold medals in five different events, appearing in five Games to 1980?

**13** At which sport did Paul Elvstrom of Denmark win four individual gold medals?

**14** Which two countries have each won three gold medals at soccer?

**15** Which Briton has won three equestrian gold medals?

**16** Who won both the Alpine Skiing Slalom and Grand Slalom by record margins?

**17** Which German showjumper won four Olympic team gold medals and one individual gold medal?

**18** Who won the 100 metres in 1948, and the 110 metres hurdles in 1952?

**19** Bob Beamon achieved his world record long jump in 1968 with which of his six jumps?

**20** At which sport did Gert Fredriksson of Sweden win six gold medals?

**1** In which event did Charlie Spedding win the bronze medal in the 1984 Olympic Games?

**2** Which football club does Sebastian Coe support — a) Loughborough Town  b) Sheffield United or c) Chelsea?

**3** Which British runner dropped out of the 1984 Olympic 1500 metres final?

**4** What is the equivalent race, in miles, to the 10 000 metres?

**5** Which one of these events is *not* part of the Olympic decathalon: 100 metres, pole vault, 400 metres hurdles, discus, javelin?

**6** Which Olympic gold medallist has been a leading organizer of the London marathon?

**7** Who was Great Britain's silver medallist in the 1984 Olympic 100 metres hurdles?

**8** Who was the Czech athlete who won the women's 400 metres and 800 metres gold medals in the 1983 world championships?

**9** Where did Jurgen Straub come between Seb Coe and Steve Ovett?

**10** Who finished second to Sebastian Coe in the 1986 European Championship 800 metres?

**11** Which of these was *not* a women's Olympic event for the first time in 1984 — 3000 metres, 400 metres hurdles, marathon, 4 x 400 metres relay?

**12** Who won the 1984 London Marathon nine months after giving birth to a son?

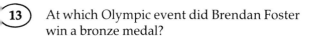

**13** At which Olympic event did Brendan Foster win a bronze medal?

**14** Whom did European gold medallist Jean Desforges marry?

**15** Which British world track record-holder later read the news on television and became an MP?

**16** This is the last bend of the Commonwealth Games 10 000 metres at Edinburgh, 1970 — who won?

**17** Who was the world record-holder at 110 metres hurdles who became an American footballer?

**18** Who was Great Britain's best-placed athlete in the 1984 Olympic Games heptathalon?

**19** Great Britain's only gold medal in the 1971 European Championships was in the 400 metres — who won it?

**20** How many times is the water jumped in the 3000 metres steeplechase?

**(1)** Who were the four men to defeat the man on the right in the photograph?

**(2)** Who lost in the 1983 cricket World Cup Final?

**(3)** Who left his world featherweight title in the Las Vegas heat in June 1986?

**(4)** Who beat the holder of the title, Steve Davis, 10–1 in the 1982 world professional snooker championships?

**(5)** Who lost to Steava Bucharest in the 1986 European Cup Final — and could not even score in the penalty shoot-out?

**(6)** Who was the Australian athlete who broke 11 world records in the 1960s but never won a major gold medal?

**(7)** Who lost to Southampton in the 1976 FA Cup Final?

**(8)** Who was the 'best pound-for-pound boxer in the world' who lost his title to Lloyd Honeyghan in 1986?

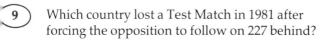

**9** Which country lost a Test Match in 1981 after forcing the opposition to follow on 227 behind?

**10** Which horse lost to *Red Rum* after leading nearly all the way in the 1973 Grand National?

**11** Who lost to Walsall in the most famous soccer giant-killing act of all in 1933?

**12** Who was the only man to lose world heavyweight title fights to both Floyd Patterson and Muhammad Ali?

**13** Who is the former Wimbledon men's singles champion who challenged Billie-Jean King and lost?

**14** Who was disqualified in the Olympic marathon in 1908 after he had been helped across the line?

**15** Who lost to North Korea in the 1966 World Cup Finals?

**16** Who was the French tennis player who was in the Wimbledon women's doubles six times between 1965 and 1975 and lost them all?

**17** Who lost to *Brigadier Gerard* in the 1971 2000 Guineas?

**18** Who lost his world boxing title at Earls Court in 1951, after having been unbeaten for eight years?

**19** Who was the bowler whom Gary Sobers hit for six sixes in one over?

**20** Who lost his job to Bobby Ferguson in 1986?

**1** Where would a player use an implement with a swan neck?

**2** Where is Bramall Lane?

**3** Where was England cricket captain Ted Dexter born?

**4** Where do the American footballers the Seahawks come from?

**5** Where did Erika Roe streak to fame —
a) Twickenham  b) Old Trafford or c) Lord's?

**6** Where is the Cosford indoor athletics stadium?

**7** Where is the US Masters golf tournament held?

**8** Where were the 1964 and 1976 winter Olympic Games held?

**9** Where is the Rowley Mile?

**10** Where is England's best-known rifle range?

**11** Where was Bobby Moore arrested and accused falsely of stealing jewellery in 1970?

**12** Where were the US Open tennis championships held from 1967 to 1977?

**13** Where did England play their first home international soccer and rugby union matches?

**14** Where in the United States is the Robert F. Kennedy Memorial Stadium?

**15** Where are the Devil's Dyke and the Derby Bank?

**16** Where are the Azteca and Olimpico stadiums?

**17** Where do horses race on the Roodee?

**18** Where do Dundee United play their home games?

**19** Who is this man, and where did he win his world boxing crown?

**20** Where was Olympic champion Eric Liddell, whose story was told in the film *Chariots of Fire*, born?

**1** Who broke the world record for the women's javelin in 1986?

**2** Which British Olympic champion runner has a middle name of Newbold?

**3** Who was the world, European and Commonwealth champion who failed to win the Olympic gold in 1984?

**4** Which road is associated with Roger Bannister's first four-minute mile?

**5** Who won the 1974 Commonwealth Games 1500 metres in world record time?

**6** Which former world record holder finished last in the Olympic 5000 metres final in Los Angeles 1984?

**7** Who won the women's world cross-country championship in 1985?

**8** Who won 12 Olympic medals and made his last Olympic appearance as torchbearer at Helsinki in 1952?

**9** This man missed immortality by 46 days. Who is he and in what was he too late?

**10** Who was the Russian sprinter who won European and Olympic gold medals in the 1970s?

**11** Which versatile champion is rarely known by his Christian names of Francis Morgan?

**12** Which high jumper, when competing in the English Schools Championships in 1983, set a British record for his event?

**13** Who was the 5ft 6in, bespectacled British runner who won European championships each side of the Second World War and held the world mile record?

**14** Who won the 1983 world 10 000 metres championship and followed it with the Olympic title?

**15** Which New Zealander, who won Olympic bronze medals at 1500 and 5000 metres, won the New York marathon in 1983?

**16** In which event was Yuriy Syedikh (USSR) an outstanding champion?

**17** Which marathon champion collapsed before the finish when winning easily in the Commonwealth Games of 1954?

**18** Who was the British athlete who, three weeks after Bannister ran a four-minute mile, became the first woman to break five minutes?

**19** Who beat Vladimir Kuts and broke the world 5000 metres record before 40 000 White City spectators and 15 million TV viewers?

**20** Who broke the world records for 3000, 5000 and 10 000 metres, and the 3000 metres steeplechase, in less than three months in 1978?

**1** Who was the first German to win the Wimbledon men's singles title?

**2** In which sport is Geoff Hunt a multiple champion?

**3** Where are the US Open tennis championships held?

**4** In which year did Virginia Wade win the Wimbledon singles championship?

**5** In which international competition was Dwight F. Davis on the first winning side?

**6** Who won the men's European badminton championship for the third successive year in 1980?

**7** Which racquet sport was invented by Major Walter Clopton Wingfield?

**8** Which country has won the Uber Cup — the ladies' badminton championship — most often?

**9** In which sport do ladies' teams contest the Corbillion Cup?

**10** What is the name of the cup for the men's international badminton championship?

**11** Who ended the 5½-year unbeaten run at squash of Jahangir Khan in 1986?

**12** For which sport, known in France as *jeu de paume*, is there a court in Hampton Court Palace?

**13** Who won the men's singles at Wimbledon in 1973, when 79 professionals boycotted the championships — a) Jan Kodes b) Tony Roche or c) Stan Smith?

**14** Which cup is awarded to the winners of the international women's team championship of tennis?

**15** Which sport gets its name from the resilience of the ball?

**16** At which sport was cricketer Colin Cowdrey runner up in the amateur championship of 1952?

**17** Who won the All-England men's badminton championship from 1968 to 1974?

**18** At which sport was Johnny Leach an English world champion?

**19** Who were the 1974 men's and women's singles champions at Wimbledon who were engaged to be married?

**20** This player was three times Wimbledon singles champion and five times women's doubles champion. Who is she, and from which country did she come?

**1** Which Dutch housewife won four gold medals at the 1948 London Olympic Games?

**2** Who in 1968 became the first swimmer, man or woman, to win three individual gold medals in one Olympics?

**3** Who was the gymnast who scored a perfect mark at the 1976 Montreal Olympics?

**4** At which event was Irena Rodnina supreme?

**5** Who won the women's all-round competition (combined gymnastics exercises) in Los Angeles 1984?

**6** Who won the pentathlon in the 1972 Munich Olympics?

**7** Who is this gymnast, who won four gold medals, two silver and three bronze, and who is the multi-Olympic medallist she married?

8. Who was Great Britain's only women's long jump gold medallist?

9. Who won Olympic gold medals in 1972 for the gymnastics disciplines of beam and floor exercises?

10. Who was the last British female swimmer to win an Olympic gold medal?

11. Who won the first Olympic heptathlon (1984)?

12. Who was both the youngest and the oldest winner of the high jump?

13. Who was the multi-gold medal winner who married a 1500 metres silver medallist after the 1968 Olympics?

14. Who won Great Britain's sole women's track and field gold medal in 1984?

15. Who won two golds and a silver in the 1976 Alpine Skiing events?

16. Who was the East German girl who won four gold medals at swimming in 1976?

17. Who was the Australian sprinter who won three gold medals in 1956, and returned after retirement in 1964 to win the 400 metres?

18. In which sport was Charlotte Cooper in 1900 the first lady to win an Olympic title?

19. Nawal El Moutawakel was a golden girl in the 400 metres hurdles for which country in 1984 — a) Algeria  b) Egypt or c) Morocco?

20. The 1956 Olympic discus champion, the Czech Olga Fikotova, married the US hammer winner and changed her name to what?

**1** Which is the only horse to win the Grand National three times?

**2** Who beat David Moorcroft's 5000 metres world record in 1986?

**3** What took place at just over 15 m.p.h. on 6 May 1954?

**4** In which sport did Karin Enke set a world record of 2 min 3·42 sec for 1500 metres in the 1984 Olympic Games?

**5** Which runner, known as 'The Flying Finn', was not allowed to take part in the Los Angeles Olympics because of professionalism?

**6** Which race did Greg Lemond become the first American to win in 1986?

**7** Which Briton held the world 10 000 metres record from 1973 to 1977?

**8** Who was the last racehorse to perform the Classic Triple Crown of 2000 Guineas, Derby and St Leger?

**9** Who won the world speedway championship a record five times between 1956 and 1967?

**10** Who set a world record for 100 metres at 9·93 seconds in 1983?

**11** Who were the father and son who each held the land speed record in cars called Bluebird?

**12** *Glint of Gold* was beaten by a record ten lengths in the Derby — by which horse?

**13** Who won a record seven British titles in the men's events at the 1976 national swimming championships?

**(14)** In World Cup skiing events, who has won the most men's downhill races?

**(15)** Who was the English runner who broke the world mile record in 1957?

**(16)** The horse photographed finishing second in the Derby later won the Prix de l'Arc de Triomphe in record time, with a different jockey up. Can you name the horse and the two jockeys who rode him?

**(17)** Which site in Utah is famous for land speed record attempts?

**(18)** Who set six world athletics records in 45 minutes on 25 May 1935?

**(19)** Who is the American jockey who has won more races than any other in the world?

**(20)** Who was the last American to hold the world mile record?

**(1)** This man hit the stumps to run out the last batsman in the first-ever tied Test match — who is he?

**(2)** Which two countries beat England in Test matches in the 1986 season?

**(3)** What is the highest ever individual Test innings, and who scored it?

**(4)** For which county did England captain Bob Willis make his debut?

**(5)** Where did Ian Botham score 149 not out against Australia in 1981?

**(6)** Who scored a century for Australia in the Centenary Test at Melbourne?

**(7)** Who were the two England batsmen who were the first pair to score double centuries in one Test match innings, at Madras in 1984–5?

**8** In the tied Test match in Brisbane, who took 11 wickets for Australia?

**9** Which England captain was the first player to be given out 'obstructing the field' in a Test match?

**10** How many wickets did Australian bowler Bob Massie take on his first Test debut at Lord's in 1972?

**11** Who was about to play for Gloucestershire in 1981 when summoned to play for Australia in the Old Trafford Test?

**12** Who replaced Tom Cartwright in the England tour party for South Africa in 1968–9?

**13** Why did Rick McCosker have particular reason to remember the Melbourne Centenary Test?

**14** Who scored the first Test century scored in Antigua — a) Viv Richards b) Peter Willey or c) Gary Sobers?

**15** Who played a famous innings of 232 for Australia at Trent Bridge in 1938?

**16** By what margin did Australia win both the first-ever Test match and the Centenary Test match?

**17** Who was the second, after Ian Botham, to score a century and take 10 wickets in a Test match?

**18** What do F. Mitchell, W.E. Midwinter, W.L. Murdoch and S.M.J. Woods have in common?

**19** Between 1968 and 1971 England played 26 successive Tests unbeaten — who played in all of them?

**20** What first did Dilip Vengsarkar achieve at Lord's in 1986?

( 1 ) In which year was the 'Stanley Matthews' FA Cup Final, won by Blackpool?

( 2 ) In which year did Randolph Turpin hold the world middleweight championship?

( 3 ) In which year did Dennis Taylor win the world professional snooker championship?

( 4 ) In which year did synchronized swimming become an Olympic event?

( 5 ) In which year did the British Lions record their first series win in New Zealand?

( 6 ) In which year did London host the Olympic Games?

( 7 ) In which year did Jim Laker take 19 Australian wickets in a Test match?

( 8 ) In which year was the first FA Cup Final played at Wembley?

( 9 ) In which year did boxers in the Olympic Games first wear headguards?

( 10 ) In which year was the first Test match?

( 11 ) In which year did Gordon Richards ride his only Derby winner?

( 12 ) In which year did Max Faulkner win the Open Golf Championship?

( 13 ) In which year was W.G. Grace born?

( 14 ) In which year did the Football League switch to the current three points for a win?

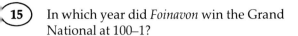

**15** In which year did *Foinavon* win the Grand National at 100–1?

**16** In which year did Chelsea win the European Cup Winners Cup?

**17** In which year did Jackie Stewart win the grand prix world drivers' championship?

**18** In which year were the Commonwealth Games held in London?

**19** In which year did Cassius Clay win the world heavyweight championship?

**20** In which year did this snooker player win the world professional title?

**1** Who is the youngest-ever world chess champion?

**2** Who was the youngest gymnast to win an Olympic gold medal?

**3** Who became the youngest world amateur snooker champion in 1980?

**4** Randolph Turpin, seen winning the world middleweight championship in 1951, beat the British champion while still too young to fight for the title. Who was that British champion?

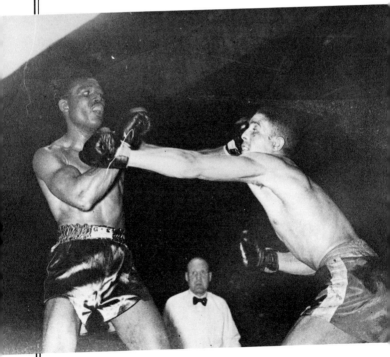

**5** Who was the oldest man to make his international soccer debut for England?

**6** Who is the youngest player to win the Wimbledon men's singles championship?

(7) Who is the oldest winner of the US Masters golf tournament — a) Jack Nicklaus  b) Gary Player or c) Arnold Palmer?

(8) Who was the youngest footballer to be capped by England?

(9) Who, in 1979, became the youngest winner of the Open golf championship for over 100 years?

(10) Who was the oldest world boxing champion, aged 44?

(11) Who is the youngest cricketer to play for England?

(12) Who, in 1980, became the youngest player to take part in the FA Cup Final?

(13) Who is the youngest man to become world heavyweight boxing champion?

(14) Who is the youngest man to win the men's world open squash championship?

(15) Who is the oldest man to play Test cricket?

(16) Who, in 1982, became the youngest player to win a singles title at the French tennis championships?

(17) At which sport did Oscar Swahn of Sweden, the oldest Olympic gold medallist, compete?

(18) Who became the youngest Test cricketer at 15 years 124 days in 1958–9?

(19) Which Frenchman was the youngest-ever European boxing champion?

(20) Who was the youngest player to be seeded at Wimbledon?

**1** What is the duration of an American football match?

**2** Who was the American golfer who had an 'army' of followers?

**3** In which sport did Wilt 'The Stilt' Chamberlain star?

**4** Which baseball player was married to Marilyn Monroe?

**5** Which team were beaten by the Chicago Bears in Superbowl XX?

**6** Who was the American golfer who holed a bunker shot at the 18th to win a major title in 1986?

**7** A kicker in American football must wear a shirt numbered between which two numbers?

**8** Which American footballer scored a record 2002 points in the National Football League?

**9** Who was the American who twice won the Olympic decathlon and appeared in a film of his life?

**10** Which basketball team has won the NBA championship most often?

**11** Which American golfer is known as the 'Walrus'?

**12** Which American President was offered terms by the NFL side Chicago Bears?

**13** How did *Liberty* end a run of well over 100 years?

**14** What were Babe Ruth's Christian names?

**15** Which American football star had a juicy role in the film *The Towering Inferno*?

**16** Who was struck by lightning in the 1975 Western Open golf tournament in Chicago?

**17** Photographed are the London Rockets playing the Wiesbaden Flyers at American football at Wembley as long ago as 1956. In which year did Channel 4 begin to televise American football regularly in Great Britain?

**18** Who is called the 'Father of American Football' because of his influence on the rules?

**19** Who was the first black golfer to represent the USA in the Ryder Cup?

**20** Whose son won the US Amateur Golf Championship in 1982?

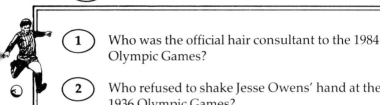

**1** Who was the official hair consultant to the 1984 Olympic Games?

**2** Who refused to shake Jesse Owens' hand at the 1936 Olympic Games?

**3** Why was a silver medal not awarded to the losing finalist in the 1952 Olympic heavyweight boxing?

**4** Which three International Olympic Committee countries were not invited to London for the 1948 Games?

**5** Who was given the 1960 100 metres swimming gold medal, despite being electronically timed a tenth of a second behind Lance Larson, who was given the silver?

**6** What salute did Tommie Smith and John Carlos perform on the winners' rostrum in 1968?

**7** Why was Boris Onischenko disqualified from the modern pentathlon in 1976?

**8** Why did Rick Demont lose his 400 metres freestyle swimming gold medal in 1972?

**9** Which sport was introduced to the Olympics in 1964 for the benefit of the host country?

**10** Which country returned to the 1952 Olympic Games after a 40-year absence?

**11** Why did Jim Thorpe forfeit his gold medals in 1912?

**12** Of what event was Spyridon Louis the appropriate winner in the first modern Olympics to please the Greek spectators?

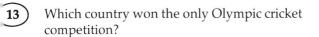

**13** Which country won the only Olympic cricket competition?

**14** Who threw his Olympic gold medal into the River Ohio?

**15** What did Abebe Bikila wear to win the 1964 marathon, which he had not worn in his 1960 victory?

**16** In which year did Great Britain win all the Olympic boxing medals?

**17** Who surprisingly beat the USSR and won the ice-hockey gold medals in 1980?

**18** What prompted the boycott of the 1980 Moscow Games?

**19** In 1896, there was a 100 metres freestyle swimming event restricted to which sort of men — a) Sailors b) Greeks or c) Cavalry officers?

**20** Who is this man, the oldest winner of the Olympic 100 metres, and what did he have to use that he had not used in previous years?

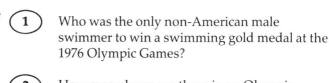

**1** Who was the only non-American male swimmer to win a swimming gold medal at the 1976 Olympic Games?

**2** How many lanes are there in an Olympic swimming pool?

**3** What was the name of Great Britain's challenger in the 1986 America's Cup?

**4** What name did Edward Heath give to his yachts?

**5** What is the distance of the University Boat Race course?

**6** In which type of craft does a competitor use a paddle with a blade on each end, as opposed to a single-bladed paddle?

**7** What had to be unbolted from its stand when the United States lost it in 1983?

**8** Oxford are seen here winning the 1967 Boat Race. What are the two bridges through which the boats must go?

**9** Which annual event began in 1839 and is the oldest of its kind in Europe?

**10** Why did Susan Brown become famous in 1981?

**11** Which woman swimmer won the 100 metres freestyle gold medal at three consecutive Olympic Games?

**12** What is the main difference between rowing and sculling?

**13** Where does the Fastnet yacht race finish?

**14** Roland Mathes and his wife won 16 Olympic swimming medals in 1968, 1972 and 1976 — who is she?

**15** In which sport was Britain's Richard Fox twice a world champion in the 1980s?

**16** What was the name of Rodney Pattison's and Iain MacDonald-Smith's Flying Dutchman class boat which won the Olympic gold medal in 1968?

**17** What was revolutionary about the America's Cup-winning yacht *Australia II*?

**18** Who was the Frenchman who won single-handed trans-Atlantic yacht races in boats called *Pen Duick*?

**19** Who was the Olympic swimming gold medallist who later played Tarzan, Buck Rogers and Flash Gordon in films?

**20** Which British oarsman won medals in five Olympic Games, and was deprived by the Second World War of an attempt at a sixth?

**1** Why was Diego Maradona's first goal against England in the 1986 World Cup the subject of controversy?

**2** Who held up a Test match for ten minutes arguing after being told he could not bat with an aluminium bat?

**3** Which team's defeat of Leeds United by a disputed 'offside' goal in 1971 cost Leeds the championship and the closing of their ground?

**4** Why did the last ball of the Australia v. New Zealand World Series Cup match on 1 February 1981 cause controversy?

**5** Who, in 1984, was the first Olympic medallist to fail a dope test — he forfeited the 10 000 metres silver?

**6** Who beat Henry Cooper in his last fight — a decision which was strongly criticized?

**7** Who was disqualified for tripping in a 1984 Olympic Games track event, but later reinstated?

**8** Which team was knocked out of the 1984–5 European Cup Winners Cup after winning a tie but being forced to replay it because of a missile thrown by a spectator?

**9** Who was captain of the English cricket team in the 'bodyline' series in Australia?

**10** In which sport did an official's decision to add three seconds to the playing time lose one team Olympic gold medals?

**11** Who was suspended for his part in a betting and bribes scandal and returned to be leading scorer in the 1982 World Cup finals?

**12** What is the name of the Argentine captain seen here being sent off in the 1966 World Cup at Wembley?

**13** Who was sent off amid controversy in the 1985 FA Cup Final?

**14** Who lost his job as England cricket captain as a result of his part in the formation of World Series Cricket?

**15** What name was given to the Chicago White Sox after losing the 1919 World Series in suspicious circumstances?

**16** Who won the Olympic gold medal in the 1908 400 metres when the other finalists refused to take part in a rerun?

**17** Who was the winner in the famous 'Battle of the Long Count' for the heavyweight championship of the world?

**18** Which team won the 1932 FA Cup Final with the help of a goal scored after many thought the ball had gone over the goal-line?

**19** Which country sent two ice hockey teams to the 1948 Olympics, of which one played but neither was included in the placings because of commercial sponsorship?

**20** Whose suspension led to over 70 members of the Association of Tennis Professionals boycotting Wimbledon in 1973?

**1** In billiards, a cannon is worth how many points?

**2** How many players are there in a netball team?

**3** What is the maximum number of seconds a boxer is allowed in his corner under BBBC rules?

**4** How many pawns are on a chessboard at the start of a game?

**5** In his final Test innings how many runs did Donald Bradman score?

**6** Photographed are the 1984 Olympic ice-dance champions. How many of their 18 marks (nine for technical impression and nine for artistic presentation) were a maximum of 6·0?

7. How many players are there on the court during a volleyball match?

8. How many darts are necessary to 'check out' from 301?

9. How many of Frank Bruno's first 30 fights lasted the distance?

10. How many overs are there in a Benson & Hedges Cup innings?

11. How many golf balls are there on the moon?

12. How many laps are there in the Indianapolis 500?

13. How many years were there between Ken Rosewall's first and last Wimbledon singles finals?

14. How many teams are there in the two conferences of the National Football League?

15. How many counters are there on a backgammon board at the start of a game?

16. How many of Sonny Liston's four world heavyweight title fights ended in the first round?

17. How many days did Brian Clough remain as Leeds United manager — a) 10  b) 44 or c) 365?

18. How many pots must be made to achieve a maximum break of 147 at snooker?

19. How many nations have won soccer's World Cup once only?

20. How many innings are there in a normal American professional baseball match?

**1** Who took part in the world chess championship match, half of which was held in England in 1986?

**2** Who collected 29 scores of six in the world ice-dance championships in Canada in 1984?

**3** Who was the first player to win the world snooker championship at Sheffield's Crucible Theatre twice?

**4** Who, in 1978, became the first world professional darts champion?

**5** Who were the two players beaten in the final by Alex Higgins in his two world professional snooker championship victories?

**6** On which apparatus did Olga Korbut win her only individual world championship?

**7** Which English badminton player (awarded the MBE in 1976) won eight English national singles titles between 1969 and 1981?

**8** In which game did Deller succeed Wilson as world champion in 1983?

**9** Who did Bobby Fischer beat to win the world chess championship?

**10** Who are the only brothers to win the world snooker championship?

**11** Who won the first world open championship at squash in 1976 — a) Jonah Barrington  b) Geoff Hunt or c) Jahangir Khan?

**12** Who were the English twins who won the world ladies' doubles table tennis championships when they were 17 years old?

**13** Who won £102 000 for a nine-dart 'check-out' in the world match-play championships in 1984?

**14** Lasker, Capablanca and Euwe were all world champions at which game?

**15** Who won 16 British open squash championships in succession from 1961 to 1976?

**16** Who was the 1986 world professional snooker champion pictured here, and by what score did he beat Steve Davis in the final?

**17** Who won the Australian professional snooker championship in 1985?

**18** At which sport have Danes Morten Frost and Lene Koppen been recent champions?

**19** Who was the first overseas player to win the *News of the World* darts championship?

**20** Who succeeded Joe Davis as world professional snooker champion?

**(1)** Photographed is a captain of Wales who, in 1973, set up a famous try for another Welsh captain by means of brilliant side-steps near his own line. Who is he, who scored the try and what was the match?

**(2)** What is the nickname of the Australian Rugby League side?

**(3)** According to legend who, at Rugby School, picked up the ball and started rugby football?

**(4)** Who was the pioneer Rugby League television commentator who died in 1986?

**(5)** What emblem is worn by the All Blacks on their shirts?

**(6)** Which rugby union player scored most points for England?

**7** Why was the 1973 Five Nations Championship remarkable?

**8** Which Rugby League player scored the most points in a career?

**9** In which town are the headquarters of the Rugby League?

**10** Who, in 1966, was the last Scot to captain the British Lions?

**11** Which Irish divisional side registered a famous victory over the All Blacks in 1978?

**12** Which British Lion was a junior tennis champion?

**13** Which side pulled off a shock in the 1983 Rugby League Challenge Cup Final, beating Hull?

**14** What are the colours of the Barbarians' shirts?

**15** Which Rugby League side is nicknamed 'The Chemics'?

**16** In rugby union, who captained the last South African Springbok tour to the British Isles?

**17** Who played for Newport, Wales and the British Lions at union, Salford, Wales and Great Britain at League?

**18** Which rugby union star joined Bradford Northern in the 1985–6 season, but was early on dogged by injury?

**19** Who were the last winners of the Olympic championship at rugby union?

**20** Which Rugby League team play at the Boulevard?

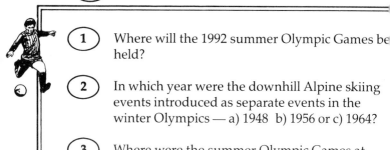

1. Where will the 1992 summer Olympic Games be held?

2. In which year were the downhill Alpine skiing events introduced as separate events in the winter Olympics — a) 1948 b) 1956 or c) 1964?

3. Where were the summer Olympic Games at which there was worry beforehand about the high altitude?

4. In which year were the only Olympic Games held in Australia?

5. Where did Alan Wells win his gold medal?

6. In which year were the first modern Olympic Games held?

7. When did England's Duncan Goodhew win a swimming gold medal?

8. In which country are the headquarters of the International Olympic Committee?

9. Which Latin American city was the first to host an Olympic Games?

10. When was the first women's Olympic marathon run?

11. Apart from Athens, London and Los Angeles, which city has hosted two summer Olympic Games?

12. When was polo last played at the Olympic Games — a) 1932 b) 1936 or c)1940?

13. Which winter Olympic venue was famous for the assassination of Archduke Ferdinand which precipitated the First World War?

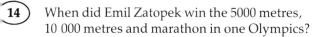

**14** When did Emil Zatopek win the 5000 metres, 10 000 metres and marathon in one Olympics?

**15** Where were the cancelled 1940 summer Games first to have been held?

**16** Photographed is Maureen Gardner who failed by inches to win gold for Great Britain in the hurdles, and consoled herself by marrying the British coach, Geoff Dyson. When and where is this race?

**17** When did Great Britain last win a medal at hockey?

**18** Where was the opening ceremony interrupted by a German girl in a flowing white robe calling herself an 'angel of peace'?

**19** When did Princess Anne compete in the Olympics?

**20** Where were the 1956 equestrian events held when quarantine problems precluded Melbourne?

**1** On which French racecourse is the Prix de l'Arc de Triomphe run?

**2** In which sport would a fancier require a loft, a transporter crate and a printing clock?

**3** Which horse was fourth in the 1986 Breeders Cup Turf race in Santa Anita, California?

**4** In horse racing, at what age does a filly become a mare?

**5** This is perhaps the greatest-ever steeplechaser, winner of three successive Gold Cups in the 1960s. Who is he and who rode him?

**6** In which direction are greyhound races run in Britain — clockwise or anti-clockwise?

**7** Which horse, owned by the Queen Mother and ridden by Dick Francis, spreadeagled itself when about to win the Grand National?

8) Which racecourse now stages the Lincolnshire Handicap?

9) Which two horse races make up the gambling medium called the Autumn Double?

10) For which of the five Classic horse races are fillies eligible?

11) In which sport does a slipper release two dogs to chase a hare?

12) Which racers are descended from *Columba livia, Columba palumbus* or *Columba oenas*?

13) Which racers are descended from the *Darley Arabian, Byerley Turk* or *Godolphin Barb*?

14) Which famous greyhound was the only one to win the English Greyhound Derby twice?

15) What is the name of the best-known Irish racecourse, near Dublin?

16) Why is 1 January a significant date for thoroughbred racehorses?

17) In British greyhound racing, which colour jacket is worn by the dog in trap 2?

18) Who was the last horse to win both the Cheltenham Gold Cup and the Grand National?

19) Which three events form the Triple Crown in United States horse racing?

20) If, in harness racing, a horse moving both left legs together, then both right, is called a pacer, what is a horse called who moves near-fore with off-hind and vice-versa?

**1** What was the name of the trophy which was awarded outright to Brazil and replaced by the FIFA World Cup?

**2** Which two countries are three-times winners of the World Cup?

**3** Who scored the first goal in the 1986 World Cup Final?

**4** Which country won the first World Cup?

**5** Which team finally eliminated England in 1974?

**6** Which is the only country to host the World Cup finals twice?

**7** Who has scored most goals (13) in one World Cup finals tournament?

**8** Apart from Italy, who beat West Germany in the 1982 finals?

**9** Who did Brazil beat in the 1962 World Cup Final?

**10** Who scored the fastest goal in a match of the World Cup finals?

**11** What was the name of the dog who discovered the World Cup in a garden in 1966?

**12** In 1986, which three teams won quarter-final matches on the penalty shoot-out?

**13** Who scored the Northern Ireland goal which beat Spain in the 1982 finals?

**14** Who was the last player to score against Wales in a World Cup finals tournament?

**15** In which year did England, Scotland, Wales and Northern Ireland all get to the World Cup finals?

**16** Which player scored four goals in one match in the 1986 finals?

**17** The man shown here with the ball played in four World Cup finals tournaments and scored in each — who is he?

**18** Before Peter Shilton, who was the last player to keep goal for England in a World Cup finals tournament?

**19** Before Gordon Strachan, who was the last player to score for Scotland in a World Cup finals tournament?

**20** In which year was the World Cup won without there being a World Cup Final?

**1** Which trophy was sponsored by Littlewoods in 1986, taking over from the Milk Marketing Board?

**2** Which trophy is awarded to the winners of Australia's first-class inter-state cricket competition?

**3** Which trophy is contested by male golfers of Europe and the United States?

**4** For which rugby union trophy do England and Scotland compete?

**5** Which trophy is awarded to the best player in the Rugby League Challenge Cup final?

**6** Which trophy is contested by the Football League and FA Cup winners?

**7** This footballer is seen registering the first Wembley Cup Final hat-trick for 20 years — in which trophy?

8. Which trophy is contested by teams of women golfers representing Great Britain and the USA?

9. Which trophy for crown green bowlers takes its name from the hotel in Blackpool at which it is played?

10. Which one-day cricket trophy was originally the Gillette Cup?

11. Which trophy is contested by national teams for the men's world table tennis championship?

12. Which trophy is awarded to the winners of the Middlesex seven-a-side rugby union tournament?

13. Which soccer trophy was the inspiration of Gabriel Hanot, a journalist on the Paris newspaper *L'Equipe*?

14. Which trophy is awarded to the winner of Australia's most important horse race?

15. Which trophy do Australia and the West Indies contest at cricket?

16. Which trophy do Oxford and Cambridge Universities contest at rugby?

17. Which trophy, donated in 1895, is contested by the highest-placed clubs in Canada's National Hockey League?

18. Which trophy is contested at Altcar and is the principal trophy in coursing?

19. Which trophy is won by the winning crew in the main event for eights at Henley Royal Regatta?

20. Which trophy is awarded to the winner of the oldest sculling race in the world?

**1** Which team has won the English Football League championship most often?

**2** Who were European, world and 1984 Olympic ice dance champions?

**3** Who has won the world professional darts championship most often?

**4** Who won a record 20 Wimbledon championships?

**5** Who was British champion jockey a record 26 times — a) Fred Archer  b) Lester Piggott or c) Gordon Richards?

**6** Who held the world long jump record, played in the FA Cup Final and opened for England at cricket?

**7** Who was the last driver to win the Formula 1 drivers' championship in successive years?

**8** Who is the only Briton to win the world, European and Olympic figure skating championships in the same year?

**9** Who held three world boxing titles at different weights simultaneously in the 1930s?

**10** Which cricketing county won the English County Championship seven times consecutively in the 1950s?

**11** Who trained nine world boxing champions, including Muhammad Ali and Sugar Ray Leonard?

**12** Who was the first person to win the Badminton horse trials four times?

**13** The player on the right scored the final League goal in a double-winning season. Who is he?

**14** What is the surname of the brother and sister who each won the combined World Cup skiing championship in 1980?

**15** Which horse won the Cheltenham Gold Cup in 1964, 1965 and 1966?

**16** Who was the last player to be capped by England in both soccer and cricket?

**17** Which motor racing driver has won the British Grand Prix most often?

**18** Which Australian golfer won the British Open three times consecutively in the 1950s, and five times in all?

**19** Who was the England cricket captain who was also an Olympic boxing champion?

**20** Who was the first woman tennis player to win the Grand Slam (the four major championships in one year)?

**1** Which cricketer scored most first-class runs in a career?

**2** Which Football League team was the first to score 100 points in a season?

**3** Photographed are three Scottish internationals, but their League club has established a record sequence of victories in a major competition in England. What was it, and who are they?

**4** Who won the Open twice in succession in 1971 and 1972?

**5** Which British soccer player was the first to achieve 1000 first-class appearances?

**6** Which British soccer player was the first to achieve 100 international appearances?

(7) Who has scored the most centuries in Test cricket?

(8) How many Football League teams have achieved the League and FA Cup double?

(9) Who is the only pre-tournament Wimbledon qualifier to reach the semi-finals?

(10) Who scored most goals in a Football League match?

(11) Who, between 1964 and 1979, won a record 69 rugby union caps for Ireland?

(12) Which cricketer, excluding wicket-keepers, took most catches in Test matches?

(13) By which record score for an FA Cup tie did Preston North End beat Hyde in 1887?

(14) Which American football player holds the record for the most appearances in the NFL?

(15) Who is the only man to perform the Grand Slam of lawn tennis twice?

(16) Which cricketer took over 300 wickets in the 1928 English summer?

(17) Who scored most points in a career in rugby union?

(18) Who scored the most goals in the Football League, but was never capped?

(19) Which tennis player has played in the most Davis Cup rubbers?

(20) Who, in 1983, became the first bowler to take seven wickets in a one-day international?

**1** By what name was the triple jump formerly known?

**2** In which event did Jozef Szmidt of Poland win the gold medal in 1960 and 1964?

**3** Which Welshman jumped to a gold medal in the rain at Tokyo?

**4** What was Britain's long jump winner Mary Rand's maiden name?

**5** What is the last event in the Olympic decathlon?

**6** Who flopped famously in the high jump but still won a gold medal?

**7** Viktor Saneyev's silver medal in the 1980 triple jump was not good enough for him to equal which record?

**8** Who was the long jump gold medallist whom Mary Peters just beat in the 1972 pentathlon?

**9** Which two gold medallists were men's and women's team mangers of the 1984 British team in Los Angeles?

**10** In which event did Americans John Thomas and John Rambo win medals in 1960 and 1964?

**11** Who was second to Daley Thompson in the 1984 decathlon?

**12** How was 1960 decathlon winner Rafer Johnson connected with the 1984 Olympics?

**13** What did British women high jumpers achieve in the Olympics between 1936 and 1960?

**14** This is the 1984 women's Olympic javelin champion; a teammate finished third. Who are they, and where did they finish in the 1980 Olympic javelin final?

**15** How many of the men's and women's throwing events were won by United States athletes in 1984 — a) none  b) one or c) six?

**16** In the 1960s, Irena Press (USSR) won a hurdles gold medal, but in which two events did her sister Tamara strike gold?

**17** Which field event, discontinued in 1920, saw Great Britain win all three events in 1908?

**18** Who was 'The Vaulting Vicar', the American preacher who twice won the pole vault in the 1950s?

**19** How was Imre Nemeth, the 1948 hammer winner, connected with the javelin in 1976?

**20** How is the winning javelin throw of Matti Jarvinen in 1932 commemorated at the Olympic stadium in Helsinki?

(1) Who is this man, the only world champion on both two wheels and four?

(2) Who wears a yellow jersey in France's most popular sporting event?

(3) Who shredded a tyre in Adelaide in 1986 and lost the grand prix world drivers' championship?

(4) At which sport was Reg Harris famous?

(5) Who founded the Lotus Engineering Company and brought many innovations to the grand prix car?

(6) What nationality is the multiple Tour de France winner Eddie Merckx?

(7) Which sport, which had a tremendous boom among children in 1977, combined principles of surfing and roller skating?

**8** Who won 14 Isle of Man TT races between 1961 and 1979?

**9** Which one of these racing drivers was not killed on the track: Piers Courage, Graham Hill, Jim Clark, Ronnie Peterson?

**10** What does a hot-rodder mean by 'snowballs'?

**11** Which sport is governed internationally by the IRSF?

**12** What nationality was Denny Hulme, world drivers' champion in 1967?

**13** Which was the first British car to win the world constructors' championship?

**14** Who was the 350cc world motorcycling champion for the seven years 1968 to 1974?

**15** Which English motorcyclist was world champion in both 350cc and 500cc classes in 1951?

**16** Who was the second Briton to win the world drivers' championship?

**17** Who won the world motorcycling 125cc title five times and the 250cc title three times between 1955 and 1960?

**18** Who was the Belgian who was 500cc moto-cross world champion five times between 1971 and 1976?

**19** Which Briton won the world sidecar championship in 1977?

**20** At which sport were Australians Lionel van Praag and Bluey Wilkinson world champions in the 1930s?

**1** Why is Munich 1958 remembered with sorrow by football supporters?

**2** Who was the assistant manager of the England cricket team who died during the 1981–2 West Indies tour?

**3** Who was the tennis champion who was first to perform the ladies' grand slam, but who died of cancer when only 35?

**4** Where was soccer's worst disaster, with 300 killed during an Olympic qualifying game in 1964?

**5** In which race did several people lose their lives by drowning in 1979?

**6** Who was resuscitated on the pitch after being felled by a bouncer in a Test match against England in 1975?

**7** Which horse won the Champion Hurdle and the Cheltenham Gold Cup but died when falling in a race overseas?

**8** Who kept goal in an FA Cup Final in 1956 with a broken neck?

**9** Who was the national soccer manager who died after a World Cup qualifying match in 1985?

**10** Which British motor racing champion died in a plane crash in 1975?

**11** Which British boxing champion died after losing a world title fight in 1980?

**12** Who was the British athlete who died of cancer in 1969, a year after winning an Olympic silver medal?

**13**  Which Olympic 1500 metres champion was killed when he fell under a New York subway car?

**14**  At which football ground was there a stampede, causing 66 deaths in 1971?

**15**  Who was the Spurs and Scotland inside forward killed by lightning?

**16**  Who was the world heavyweight champion who was killed in a plane crash in 1969?

**17**  Who scored 64 goals in his first 63 Football League games in the 1950s, and then had a leg amputated after colliding with a goalie?

**18**  Who was the Olympic boxing champion, amateur international footballer and England cricket captain who was drowned trying to save his father in a shipping accident?

**19**  Who was middleweight champion of the world when shot by a jealous ranch hand?

**20**  Both these kings of speed were killed in accidents — who are they?

**1** Which team, in 1970, sang about their desire to be 'Back Home'?

**2** Which county has won cricket's County Championship most often?

**3** Which team did the Los Angeles Raiders beat 38—9 in Superbowl XVIII in 1984?

**4** Which team paid a lot of money for Pele in 1975?

**5** Which county cricket club includes the Prince of Wales' feathers in its badge — a) Gloucestershire b) Glamorgan or c) Surrey?

**6** Which soccer team was the first from England to qualify for the European Cup, but was forbidden to take part by the Football League?

**7** This horse and jockey partnership both overcame adversity and their story was told in a feature film. Who played the jockey?

8) Which team included Jim McMahon, Walter Payton, Mike Singletary and William Perry to win a 1986 championship?

9) Which team is the only one to take the FA Cup out of England?

10) Which cricket team was 0 runs for 4 wickets in a Test match in 1952?

11) Which English soccer team was banned from Europe for two years in 1975 because of crowd violence?

12) Which rugby union team supplied Dusty Hare, Paul Dodge and Clive Woodward simultaneously to England?

13) Which team plays on Gay Meadows?

14) Which team in the NFL has black and orange stripes on its helmet?

15) Which team has won the European Cup most often?

16) Which team plays at the Astrodome on Astroturf?

17) Which team won the women's volleyball gold medals at the 1984 Olympic Games?

18) Which soccer team began life as Saint Domingo Church Sunday School Club?

19) Which teams contest the Eton wall game annually on the nearest Saturday to St Andrew's Day?

20) Which team won baseball's World Series in 1986?

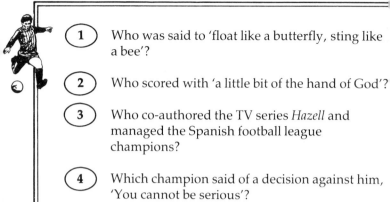

**1** Who was said to 'float like a butterfly, sting like a bee'?

**2** Who scored with 'a little bit of the hand of God'?

**3** Who co-authored the TV series *Hazell* and managed the Spanish football league champions?

**4** Which champion said of a decision against him, 'You cannot be serious'?

**5** Who kept asking Harry if he knew what he meant?

**6** Who said, 'I don't think football's a matter of life and death. It's more important than that'?

**7** Why was cricketer Chris Old nicknamed Chilly?

**8** Who admitted taking drugs and was suspended for not admitting it earlier?

**9** Which cricketer was told in 1932/33 to 'leave our bloody flies alone'?

**10** Who continually thanked Mr Eastwood, but finally fell out with him?

**11** What was the prominent facial feature that earned Argentine World Cup manager Carlos Bilardo his nickname?

**12** Whose 1986 diary was published under the title *So Near and Yet So Far*?

**13** For which county did the current Bishop of Liverpool play cricket?

**14** What relationship is Ryan O'Neal to John McEnroe's son?

**15** Who featured in a calypso as 'those little pals of mine'?

**16** Whose statement, 'We can bounce back' was a headline in the 1986 newspaper which, in its stop press, announced his sacking?

**17** The boxer on the left in the photograph called the boxer on the right 'a Master of Disaster.' Who are they?

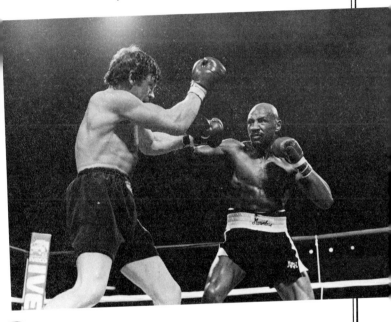

**18** Which cricketer became chairman of Melchester Rovers, the Rovers of 'Roy of the Rovers'?

**19** Who said, 'I didn't realise they cared so much' when the crowd cheered a classic performance?

**20** Which Australian cricketer asked the Queen for her autograph?

(1) This is Sandy Lyle, who in 1985 became Britain's first Open champion for 16 years. But who was runner up?

(2) Who were the hockey world champions in 1986?

(3) In what capacity were Frank Chester and Harold Bird well known?

(4) Who manages former world snooker champions Steve Davis, Terry Griffiths and Dennis Taylor, among others?

(5) What sport is played at Cowdray Park?

(6) In which sport was the ball originally stuffed with boiled feathers?

7. What do the laws stipulate as the maximum width of a cricket bat?

8. In which sport is Sean Kerly a leading English player?

9. Who was eliminated by Jack Nicklaus in the 1986 World Matchplay championship?

10. In which game are there winning and losing hazards and cannons?

11. How many balls, including the cue ball, are on the table at the start of a game of snooker?

12. Which sport has an infield, an outfield, and a pitcher and catcher, called the battery?

13. Which three current first-class cricket counties have never won the County championship?

14. On which famous golf course does every hole bear the name of a plant?

15. In which Gaelic sport is the goal area called the parallelogram?

16. In which sport might your balls be red and yellow but your opponent's black and blue?

17. What is the penalty in snooker if, after potting a red, a player pots another red on his following shot?

18. How many players are there in a shinty team?

19. In which sport is the Tooting Bec Cup awarded?

20. Which sport did Julius Caesar play when touring the United States?

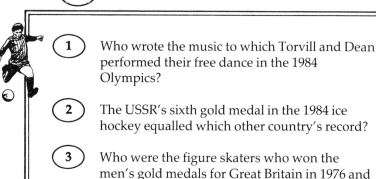

**1** Who wrote the music to which Torvill and Dean performed their free dance in the 1984 Olympics?

**2** The USSR's sixth gold medal in the 1984 ice hockey equalled which other country's record?

**3** Who were the figure skaters who won the men's gold medals for Great Britain in 1976 and 1980?

**4** Who won all five men's speed skating gold medals in the 1980 Olympics?

**5** Who skated to gold medals in 1928, 1932 and 1936, and later achieved fame as a Hollywood film star?

**6** Who won both Alpine skiing slalom gold medals in 1980?

**7** Which two sports are combined in the Olympic biathlon?

**8** Which country finished both first and second in both the two- and four-man bobsleigh in 1984?

**9** Which Swiss town has twice hosted the winter Olympics?

**10** Who, in 1984, became the first American skier to win the Olympic downhill?

**11** Who won all three men's Alpine skiing events at the 1968 Olympics?

**12** What is the surname of the US twins who finished first and second in the 1984 slalom?

**13** What is the surname of the French sisters who finished first and second in both the 1964 slaloms?

**14** How many teams are each country permitted in the four-man bobsled event?

**15** What is the skating jump named after the 1908 men's figure skating gold medallist?

**16** Which event did Tony Nash and Robin Dixon win for Great Britain in 1964?

**17** Who was the Austrian reserve in the 1980 Alpine skiing team who won the gold medal in the downhill?

**18** Which race was won in 1928 by over 13 minutes and in 1984 by less than 5 seconds?

**19** Which Nordic skiing events are judged by distance and style?

**20** This girl won Great Britain's first skating gold medal for 44 years; instead of turning professional, she went to work in the Pestalozzi village for orphans in Switzerland — who is she?

**1** Who won the Grand National in 1986?

**2** Which horse won the Grand National for the third time in 1977?

**3** On which racecourse is the Grand National run?

**4** Who was the first woman to train a Grand National winner?

**5** This is *Red Rum* on his way to victory in the 1973 Grand National in which he just beat a horse giving him 23lb. Who was the horse he beat and who rode him?

**6** Who was the jockey who overcame cancer to win the Grand National in 1981?

**7** What is the name of the road which crosses the Grand National course?

**8** How many jumps does a horse make in the Grand National?

**9** Who rode the 1962 winner, *Kilmore*, and trained the 1965 winner, *Jay Trump*?

**10** Who is the current television expert who finished second on *Carrickbeg*?

**11** Who, in 1839, fell into the water twice on a horse called *Conrad* and has been remembered at the same fence ever since?

**12** Brian Fletcher's three wins were on two horses — what did their names have in common?

**13** Who trained a record four winners between 1956 and 1976?

**14** Which outstanding chaser, owned by Miss Dorothy Paget, won in record time with 12 stone 2 pounds in 1934?

**15** Who was the owner of *Red Rum*?

**16** Why was the race in 1967 which *Foinavon* won at 100–1 remarkable?

**17** To within five, how many ran in 1929, the largest National field?

**18** What was *Arkle*'s best performance in the Grand National?

**19** Who was the well-known hairdresser who owned the winners *Ayala* in 1963 and *Rag Trade* in 1976?

**20** What was the name of the 1949 National winner tipped by the Communist newspaper *The Daily Worker* at 66–1?

**1** Which British footballer won the most international caps?

**2** Which footballer three times scored five goals in a match and in 1960–61 scored six First Division hat-tricks for Chelsea?

**3** Which British athlete took 5 seconds off the world 5000 metres record in 1982?

**4** Who, in the 1980s, became the richest sportswoman in the world?

**5** Who is the only post-Second World War cricketer to score 1000 runs before the end of May in an English season — a) Colin Cowdrey b) Glenn Turner or c) Geoff Boycott?

**6** Who has made the most international soccer appearances for Scotland?

**7** Who made the highest individual score in a Gillette Cup final?

**8** Who held the last world mile record over 4 minutes?

**9** Which was the first team to win the Football League championship three times?

**10** Who holds the record of scoring 499 in a first-class cricket match?

**11** Who scored 410 goals in 408 games for Celtic and Clydebank?

**12** Who is the chess player who had the highest ever ELO rating?

**13** Who was the tallest world heavyweight boxing champion?

**14** All four runners in the picture were world record-holders — who are they?

**15** Who is the cricketer who has played in most Test matches?

**16** What is the biggest victory in British soccer (clue: it was in the Scottish Cup)?

**17** Teofilio Stevenson was the second boxer to win three Olympic gold medals — who was the first?

**18** Who was the first footballer to be transferred for £1000?

**19** Who was the only player to win three Wimbledon championships in the same year without dropping a set — and did it twice?

**20** Which two teams have won the Scottish Cup Final by 6–1 — in 1888 and 1972?

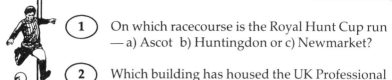

**1** On which racecourse is the Royal Hunt Cup run — a) Ascot  b) Huntingdon or c) Newmarket?

**2** Which building has housed the UK Professional (now Open) Snooker Championship since 1978?

**3** Which French circuit has held a 24-hour sports car race annually since 1923?

**4** Which city hosted the 1964 summer Olympic Games?

**5** Which riverside town annually holds races for the Silver Goblets and Diamond Sculls?

**6** Which racecourse stages the National Hunt festival meeting, which includes the Gold Cup and Champion Hurdle?

**7** This is Kua Yao-Hua in the final of the 1977 world table tennis championships; in which Midlands venue were they held?

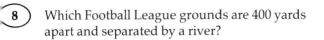

**8** Which Football League grounds are 400 yards apart and separated by a river?

**9** Which ground in Canterbury is the headquarters of Kent County Cricket Club?

**10** Which stadium staged the 1982 World Cup Final?

**11** On which course did Tony Jacklin win the 1969 Open Championship?

**12** From which Football League ground can soccer fans overlook the University Boat Race?

**13** In which stadium in Oslo did Seb Coe, Steve Ovett and Steve Cram set world mile records?

**14** On which ground did Real Madrid beat Eintracht Frankfurt 7–3 in the 1960 European Cup Final?

**15** Which country was the venue for hockey's World Cup in 1986?

**16** Which New York venue, famous for world boxing championship matches, is now in its fourth location, over Pennsylvania station?

**17** In which Paris stadium are the French tennis championships held?

**18** Which point on the French coast is nearest to Dover and often features in cross-Channel swims?

**19** Which park is the home of the San Francisco 49ers?

**20** Which Test match grounds in Auckland, New Zealand, and Calcutta, India, share a similar name?

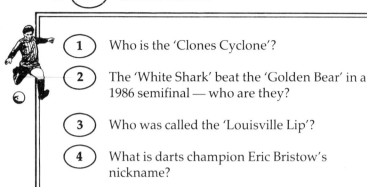

**1** Who is the 'Clones Cyclone'?

**2** The 'White Shark' beat the 'Golden Bear' in a 1986 semifinal — who are they?

**3** Who was called the 'Louisville Lip'?

**4** What is darts champion Eric Bristow's nickname?

**5** Who earned the nickname 'Superbrat'?

**6** Who are called the 'Hurricane' and the 'Whirlwind'?

**7** Who was known as 'Lynn the Leap'?

**8** Who is the tennis player who did not quite win Wimbledon, and who was called 'Muscles'?

**9** Which Football League championship-winning club is sometimes called 'The Baggies'?

**10** Edson Arantes do Nascimento shortened his name to what?

**11** Which hard-hitting batsman was known as 'The Croucher'?

**12** Who was the 'Ghost with a Hammer in his Hand'?

**13** Which speedy Olympic champion was called 'White Lightning'?

**14** Who was the 'Lion of Vienna'?

**15** Who is the cricketer known as 'Arkle'?

**16** Who was the 'Human Windmill'?

**17** Who brought frilly pants to Wimbledon and earned the nickname 'Gorgeous Gussie'?

**18** Who is this boxer and what is his nickname?

**19** Which jockey was known as 'The Head Waiter' because of his late finishing bursts?

**20** Who was the 'Clown Prince of Soccer'?

**1** Which form of football requires the largest pitch, with a maximum length of 150 yards?

**2** In rugby union, by what record international score did Ireland beat Romania in 1986?

**3** Which was Mike Channon's first professional club?

**4** Which football team plays at the Baseball Ground?

**5** Diego Maradona is pictured after Argentina's World Cup victory over England in 1986. For which two European clubs did he play between 1982 and 1986?

**6** In which form of football are there linebackers, wide receivers and tight ends?

**7** Who is the Welsh singer and comedian whose act and records strongly feature rugby?

8. Who, since the Second World War, is the only player to score six First Division hat-tricks in one season?

9. Which country won the European soccer championship in 1984?

10. Which Rugby League team plays at Wilderspool?

11. Which form of football is played in leagues called the Ivy League, Western Athletic and Big Eight?

12. What is the nickname of the Australian rugby union team — a) The Koalas b) The Wallabies or c) The Kangaroos?

13. Who was manager of Derby County when they last won the League Championship?

14. Who was the rugby player who played both union and League for England and won the television *Superstars* competition?

15. Who are the 'Scarlets' who play at Stradey Park?

16. Which is the only European football code not to have an offside rule?

17. How were Price, Windsor and Faulkner collectively known?

18. In which form of football is the Grey Cup the principal trophy?

19. Which football club plays at Firhill Park, Glasgow?

20. Who was the legendary coach of the Green Bay Packers?

**1** Who received seven 'tens' in Montreal, 1976?

**2** Who won nine gold medals in 1968 and 1972?

**3** Whose record long jump in the 1968 Olympics still stands?

**4** Who set a world record in winning the women's pentathlon at Munich?

**5** Who was the Olympic champion who first swam 100 metres in a minute and later became Hollywood's Tarzan?

**6** Show jumper Raimondo d'Inzeo competed in the most Olympic Games — how many?

**7** Who set a world track record in 1972 after falling in his race?

**8** Who is the only man since 1906 to win both the 400 and 800 metres gold medals?

**9** Who won the 1960 1500 metres by an amazing 20 yards in a new world record?

**10** Which is the only host country not to win a gold medal at its own summer Games?

**11** Who was the Scot who set a world record in winning the 200 metres breaststroke gold medal in Montreal?

**12** In which sport did Malcolm Cooper of Great Britain equal a world record in the 1984 Olympics?

**13** In which event was the only new world track event record set at the 1984 Olympics?

**14** Who was the Soviet swimmer who, in 1980, became the first man to swim 1500 metres in under 15 minutes?

**15** Who was the Ethiopian athlete who, in 1980, became the oldest track gold medallist?

**16** Who was the Soviet Olympic heavyweight weight-lifting champion who broke 80 world records in his career?

**17** A granddaughter of which multiple gold medallist carried the Olympic flame into the stadium in 1984?

**18** Who was the gymnast who won a record total of nine gold, five silver and four bronze medals?

**19** Who was the West German swimmer who broke two world records in the 1984 Olympic Games?

**20** This man won four gold medals in track and field, emulating a man who achieved the same four gold medals 48 years earlier. Who is he, whom did he emulate, and what were the four events?

**1** This is the 1980 Olympic steeplechase, won by the athlete (539) who was fourth in Munich and second in Montreal. He was later killed in an accident. Who was he?

**2** How many swimming strokes are recognized in the Olympic Games?

**3** Where were the 1986 Commonwealth Games held?

**4** What happened to the Cambridge boat before the start of the 1984 Boat Race?

**5** Who won the 1985 London marathon?

**6** Who were the two Scots to win the Formula 1 drivers' championship?

**7** At which sport was Beryl Burton a world champion?

**8** Who rode *Red Rum* in his last Grand National victory?

**9** Who won an Olympic gold medal at 1500 metres and another at the 3000 metres steeplechase?

**10** What are the three Alpine ski races?

**11** What was the name of the American yacht beaten for the America's Cup by *Australia II*?

**12** In British greyhound racing, the dog in which trap wears the black and white striped jacket?

**13** Who won the first single-handed trans-Atlantic yacht race in the ketch *Gipsy Moth IV*?

**14** Who was the New Zealander who won a 5000 metres Olympic gold medal despite a withered left arm and shoulder?

**15** Which horse won the Prix de l'Arc de Triomphe in 1986?

**16** In which respect are Alpine ski races different to Nordic ski races?

**17** In which sport are 470, Finn and Star classes?

**18** In which sport was Prince Birabonge of Siam, or B. Bira, a leading practitioner?

**19** Who was the first woman to ride in the Grand National?

**20** Who was the first jockey to ride 1000 National Hunt winners — a) Fred Winter b) Stan Mellor or c) John Francome?

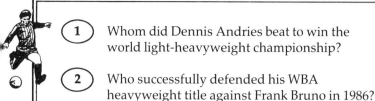

**1** Whom did Dennis Andries beat to win the world light-heavyweight championship?

**2** Who successfully defended his WBA heavyweight title against Frank Bruno in 1986?

**3** In which town did Muhammad Ali regain his title by defeating George Foreman —
a) Kinshasa, Zaire  b) Kingston, Jamaica or
c) Manila, Philippines?

**4** Which title did Hughroy Currie lose to Horace Notice in 1986?

**5** Who was knocked out by Marvin Hagler in the eleventh round of a world title fight at Las Vegas in 1986?

**6** Who was Rocky Marciano's last opponent?

**7** On whose football ground did Barry McGuigan win his world title?

**8** Which world title was Sugar Ray Robinson trying to win when he was forced to retire, when in front, from heat exhaustion?

**9** Who stopped Charlie Magri in 1986 to become European flyweight champion?

**10** Who was played by Paul Newman in the film *Somebody Up There Likes Me*?

**11** In which round was Jack Johnson knocked out when he lost his title to Jess Willard?

**12** Who beat Tommy Jackson, Pete Rademacher and Roy Harris in world heavyweight title fights?

**13** Who is the Italian boxer who beat Ubaldo Sacco to win the WBA light-welterweight title in 1986?

**(14)** What did Gene Tunney's and Rocky Marciano's careers have in common?

**(15)** Who beat Aleksei Kisselyov to win a middleweight title in 1968?

**(16)** Who was the first challenger to Marvin Hagler's middleweight title to take him the distance?

**(17)** Jim Watt is shown here defending his world lightweight championship in Glasgow. Who was the only boxer to defeat him in Scotland?

**(18)** How did Scotsman Benny Lynch lose his world flyweight championship?

**(19)** Before Leon and Michael Spinks, who were the only brothers to take part in world heavyweight title fights?

**(20)** Which father and son have held the British heavyweight championship since the Second World War?

(1) In which sport would you play on a diamond?

(2) In which sport might the Montreal Canadiens meet the Toronto Maple Leafs?

(3) In which sport might you jerk and snatch?

(4) In which sport is Joe Montana a star?

(5) In which sport did the Baltimore Bays meet the Los Angeles Toros?

(6) In which sport did this man captain England from 1903 to 1908?

**7** In which sport is a score of 26 sometimes referred to as 'bed and breakfast'?

**8** In which sport might you perform a randy on a bed?

**9** In which sport might you use an axel and a lutz?

**10** In which sport might the Baltimore Orioles meet the Detroit Tigers?

**11** In which sport did Gillian Sheen win an Olympic gold medal for Great Britain?

**12** In which sport might you use plugs, shot and a gaff?

**13** In which sport might you perform a plough turn, a steam turn and a christiana?

**14** In which sport did *Weatherley* beat *Gretel* in 1962?

**15** In which sport might the Boston Celtics meet the Los Angeles Lakers?

**16** In which sport might you brush a house for a stone?

**17** In which sport did *Oxo, Anglo* and *L'Escargot* shine?

**18** In which sport was Val Robinson a famous performer?

**19** In which sport is the Federation Internationale des Luttes Amateurs the ruling body?

**20** In which sport did Angelo Parisi win Olympic medals for both Great Britain and France in the 1970s and 1980s?

# THE ANSWERS

## 1 · C · BOXING

1. Henry Cooper
2. Sugar Ray Robinson
3. Joe Louis
4. Sonny Liston
5. Bob Fitzsimmons
6. Lloyd Honeyghan
7. John L. Sullivan
8. Muhammad Ali and Joe Frazier
9. Leon and Michael Spinks
10. Jack Dempsey and Georges Carpentier
11. Finbar
12. Azumah Nelson
13. Jersey Joe Walcott
14. Maurice Hope
15. Joey Maxim
16. Ezzard Charles
17. Carlos Monzon
18. Max Schmeling
19. Marcel Cerdan
20. Eusebio Pedroza

## 2 · BS · SOCCER

1. Trevor Ford
2. Arsenal
3. Tangerine
4. Aldershot
5. Bertie Mee
6. It was the first to require a replay
7. Huddersfield Town
8. Liverpool
9. Cardiff City
10. Gary Lineker and Mark Hughes
11. Walter Winterbottom
12. Halifax Town
13. Benfica
14. Kevin Keegan
15. Bob Paisley
16. Ferenc Puskas
17. George Camsell
18. Inter-Milan
19. Dino Zoff (Italy)
20. Queen's Park and Vale of Leven

## 3 · OG · ON TRACK

1. Steve Ovett
2. Joaquim Cruz
3. Ten
4. David Hemery
5. He was born in Munich
6. Evelyn Ashford
7. Jack Lovelock
8. A watch, to check lap times
9. 800 metres
10. Harold Abrahams and Eric Liddell
11. The 110 metres hurdles
12. Maricica Puica
13. Pietro Mennea
14. From the way he pronounced his initials 'J. C.'
15. Ann Packer (later Mrs Brightwell)
16. The runners ran a lap too many
17. Mohamed Gammoudi (silver), Ian Stewart (bronze) and Lasse Viren (gold)
18. Chris Brasher
19. Fourth
20. He fell at the last barrier while disputing the lead

## 4 · RS · DERBY DAY

1. Epsom
2. *Shergar*
3. HH Aga Khan III
4. *Never Say Die* (1954)
5. Steve Donoghue
6. *The Minstrel, Hot Grove, Blushing Groom*
7. Colts carry 9 stone, fillies 8 stone 9 pounds
8. He was actually a ringer, a four-year-old called *Maccabeus*
9. *Pinza*
10. *Mahmoud* (1936)
11. Nine
12. *Rheingold*
13. Suffragette Emily Davison threw herself under the King's horse and was killed
14. *Slip Anchor*
15. They started at 100–1
16. b) 1780
17. Sir Charles Bunbury
18. *Hard Ridden*
19. Arthur Budgett
20. All were owned by Sir Victor Sassoon

## 5 · FE · CUP FINALS

1. Danny Blanchflower (1961)
2. Sunderland
3. Bert Turner
4. Bill Perry
5. West Ham United
6. Gary Lineker
7. Bolton Wanderers
8. a) Bobby Moore
9. Tottenham Hotspur
10. Everton (1966)
11. Tommy Hutchison scored for both sides and Manchester City lost the replay against Spurs
12. Bolton Wanderers: 4–3 to Blackpool
13. Leicester City
14. Brighton (1983)
15. Charlie George
16. Wanderers
17. Brian Talbot
18. Pat Rice, five; Liam Brady, three
19. Lord Kinnaird
20. Six: Stevens, Ratcliffe, Mountfield, Reid, Steven, Sharp

## 6 · W · WHO?

1. Tessa Sanderson
2. Barry McGuigan
3. Sir Gordon Richards
4. Norman Whiteside
5. Steve Cauthen
6. Henry Cooper
7. Richard Hadlee
8. Ernie Terrell
9. Dixie Dean
10. Elizabeth Taylor
11. Gary Sobers
12. Steve Cauthen
13. Jersey Joe Walcott
14. Gary Sobers
15. Pancho Gonzales and Charlie Pasarell
16. Peter Collins
17. Tiina Lillak
18. Al Jolson
19. Howard Payne
20. Dick McTaggart

## 7 · C · GOLF

1. Peter Alliss
2. Isao Aoki
3. They are the only Continental winners of the Open
4. Max Faulkner
5. Greg Norman
6. A.D. 'Bobby' Locke
7. Peter Thomson, Kel Nagle, Greg Norman (illustrated)
8. Graham Marsh
9. Bobby Jones
10. He was the first German to win it
11. Tony Jacklin
12. Ben Hogan
13. Jack Nicklaus
14. Peter Oosterhuis
15. David Graham
16. Dai Rees
17. Roberto de Vicenzo, in 1967
18. Hale Irwin
19. Fuzzy Zoeller
20. Jock Hutchison, in 1921

## 8 · BS · CRICKET

1. Marylebone Cricket Club
2. 903 for 7 dec.
3. Sussex
4. Hampshire (Greenidge and Marshall)
5. William Gilbert
6. Brisbane
7. Laxman Sivaramakrishnan
8. Derbyshire (Chesterfield)
9. Kent and England wicket-keepers: L.E.G. Ames, T.G. Evans and A.P.E. Knott
10. Foster
11. England and New Zealand
12. Tom Graveney
13. 18
14. Bill Bowes
15. Ian Botham, who beat the record of Dennis Lillee
16. The Shell Shield
17. Jeeves
18. Philadelphia
19. Australia, West Indies and India
20. He made a pair (out for 0 in both innings)

## 9 · OG · TRADITIONS

1. Great Britain. Only team manager Dick Palmer paraded, and did not carry the Union Jack as a protest against the Soviet invasion of Afghanistan
2. Baron Pierre de Coubertin
3. The five continents
4. The Duke of Edinburgh
5. Athens
6. Enriqueta Basilio was the first woman to do so
7. Greece
8. The host country's team
9. Eddie Charlton
10. 1932
11. Ed Moses
12. 776BC
13. 1936
14. Walt Disney
15. Lord Killanin
16. The most stylish boxer in the Games
17. A corner of his national flag
18. Faster, Higher, Stronger
19. Blue, yellow, black, green, red
20. Olympia, in Greece

## 10 · RS · MOTOR RACING

1. Alain Prost
2. Red
3. Jackie Stewart
4. Argentinian
5. None
6. The Le Mans 24 Hours
7. Brooklands
8. Jack Brabham
9. Lord Hesketh
10. Tyrell
11. The Indianapolis 500
12. Mike Hawthorn
13. Bentley
14. Jochen Rindt
15. Phil Hill
16. She was the first woman to drive in a world championship grand prix
17. Alberto Ascari
18. He was later disqualified
19. Goodwood
20. Roger Clark

## 11 · FE · FIRSTS

1. Joe Frazier
2. Ray Reardon
3. Celtic
4. Cliff Thorburn
5. Geoff Boycott (left) was the first to score his 100th century in a Test; Ian Botham was the first to score a century and take ten wickets in a Test
6. Floyd Patterson
7. Joan Benoit
8. Aston Villa
9. Chris Lewis
10. Dick Turpin
11. Ivan Mauger
12. 1968
13. Charles Bannerman
14. Nobody: Scotland 0 England 0
15. She was first to fail a sex test
16. b) Stanley Matthews
17. She was the first woman to swim the channel
18. The first-ever goal in an FA Cup Final
19. Willie Park
20. Alex Metreveli

## 12 · W · WHAT?

1. The Ashes
2. Three points
3. Double-one
4. The hand
5. Puissance
6. One lap to go
7. *Doublet*
8. 167
9. The Queensberry rules in boxing — he became the Marquess of Queensberry
10. A chinaman
11. The broad jump
12. A score of one over par on a hole
13. Six
14. Bridge
15. Basketball
16. Royal Ocean Racing Club
17. Albania
18. An ice-hockey puck
19. Golf courses at St Andrews
20. A stone

## 13 · C · TENNIS

1. Neale Fraser
2. Bjorn Borg
3. Moffitt
4. John and Tracy Austin
5. West Germany
6. Rosemary Casals
7. Ilie Nastase
8. Hana Mandlikova
9. Margaret Court
10. Kevin Curren and Ivan Lendl
11. Evonne Goolagong
12. Jaroslav Drobny
13. Jimmy Connors
14. Angela Mortimer, who beat Christine Truman
15. Tracy Austin
16. None
17. Manuel Santana
18. c) Donald Budge
19. Ann Jones
20. Althea Gibson

## 14 · BS · RULES

1. Bails
2. Ten feet (3·05 metres)
3. Twelve yards (11 metres)
4. Four points
5. Fourteen
6. Australian rules football
7. Four points
8. 30 seconds
9. Three feet (0·914 metres)
10. 25 yards
11. Five runs to the batsman
12. Hashmarks
13. Lacrosse
14. Eight yards wide, eight feet high (7·32x2·44 metres)
15. Four
16. Seven
17. The service line
18. Bill Alley
19. Jai alai, or pelota
20. Gaelic football

## 15 · OG · WINNERS

1. Carl Lewis
2. Teofilio Stevenson
3. Lasse Viren
4. Sebastian Coe
5. 200 metres, 400 metres, 4x400 metres relay
6. India
7. Seven — US swimmer Mark Spitz in 1972
8. Two and seven. Daley Thompson won four events in 1980 and three in 1984
9. Emil Zatopek and Dana Zatopkova in the discus
10. Al Oerter
11. Wyomia Tyus — in 1968 and 1972
12. Irena Szewinska (née Kirszenstein)
13. Yachting
14. Great Britain and Hungary
15. Richard Meade
16. Toni Sailer
17. Hans Winkler
18. Harrison Dillard
19. The first
20. Canoeing

## 16 · RS · ATHLETICS

1. The marathon
2. c) Chelsea
3. Steve Ovett
4. Six miles
5. 400 metres hurdles
6. Chris Brasher
7. Shirley Strong
8. Jarmila Kratochvilova
9. In the 1980 Olympic 1500 metres final
10. Tom McKean
11. 4x400 metres relay
12. Ingrid Kristiansen
13. 10 000 metres
14. Ron Pickering
15. Chris Chataway
16. Lachie Stewart (Scotland). Ron Clarke and Dick Taylor are the others
17. Renaldo Nehemiah
18. Judy Simpson
19. David Jenkins
20. Seven

## 17 · FE · LOSERS

1. Joe Frazier, Ken Norton, Leon Spinks, Larry Holmes; they all beat Muhammad Ali
2. West Indies
3. Barry McGuigan
4. Tony Knowles
5. Barcelona
6. Ron Clarke
7. Manchester United
8. Don Curry
9. Australia
10. *Crisp*
11. Arsenal
12. Brian London
13. Bobby Riggs
14. Dorando Pietri
15. Italy
16. Francoise Durr
17. *Mill Reef*
18. Sugar Ray Robinson
19. Malcolm Nash
20. Ron Atkinson

## 18 · W · WHERE?

1. On a snooker table — it is a rest
2. Sheffield
3. Milan, Italy
4. Seattle
5. a) Twickenham
6. Birmingham
7. Augusta, Georgia
8. Innsbruck
9. Newmarket
10. Bisley, Surrey
11. Bogota, Colombia
12. West Side Club, New York
13. Kennington Oval
14. Washington — home of the Redskins
15. Hickstead
16. Mexico City
17. Chester
18. Tannadice Park
19. Marvin Hagler, at Wembley
20. China

## 19 · C · TRACK AND FIELD

1. Fatima Whitbread
2. Sebastian Coe
3. Steve Cram
4. Iffley Road, Oxford — the track on which he ran
5. Filbert Bayi
6. David Moorcroft
7. Zola Budd
8. Paavo Nurmi
9. John Landy. He was the second man to run a mile in under four minutes
10. Valeri Borzov
11. Daley Thompson
12. Geoff Parsons
13. Sydney Wooderson
14. Alberto Cova
15. Rod Dixon
16. Hammer
17. Jim Peters
18. Diane Leather
19. Chris Chataway
20. Henry Rono

## 20 · BS · RACQUET SPORTS

1. Boris Becker
2. Squash
3. Flushing Meadow, New York
4. 1977 — Silver Jubilee Year
5. The Davis Cup
6. Fleming Delfs
7. Lawn tennis
8. Japan
9. Table tennis
10. The Thomas Cup
11. Ross Norman
12. Real tennis
13. a) Jan Kodes
14. The Federation Cup
15. Squash
16. Rackets
17. Rudi Hartono
18. Table tennis
19. Jimmy Connors and Chris Evert
20. Maria Bueno, Brazil

## 21 · OG · GREAT LADIES

1. Fanny Blankers-Koen
2. Debbie Meyer
3. Nadia Comaneci
4. Pairs figure skating
5. Mary-Lou Rettan
6. Mary Peters
7. Lyudmila Turischeva; she married Valeri Borzov
8. Mary Rand
9. Olga Korbut
10. Anita Lonsborough
11. Glynis Nunn
12. Ulrike Mayfarth (16 in 1972, 28 in 1984)
13. Vera Caslavska
14. Tessa Sanderson
15. Rosi Mittermaier
16. Kornelia Ender
17. Betty Cuthbert
18. Tennis
19. c) Morocco
20. Connolly (she married Hal Connolly)

## 22 · RS · RECORDS

1. *Red Rum*
2. Said Aouita
3. Roger Bannister ran the first four-minute mile
4. Speed skating
5. Paavo Nurmi in 1932
6. The Tour de France
7. David Bedford
8. *Nijinsky*
9. Ove Fundin
10. Calvin Smith
11. Malcolm and Donald Campbell
12. *Shergar* (1981)
13. Brian Brinkley
14. Franz Klammer
15. Derek Ibbotson
16. *Dancing Brave* (in 1986); Greville Starkey and Pat Eddery
17. The Bonneville Salt Flats
18. Jesse Owens
19. Willie Shoemaker
20. Jim Ryun

## 23 · FE · TEST MATCHES

1. Joe Solomon (West Indies)
2. India and New Zealand
3. 365 not out by Gary Sobers
4. Surrey
5. Headingley, Leeds
6. Rodney Marsh
7. Graeme Fowler and Mike Gatting
8. Alan Davidson
9. Len Hutton
10. 16
11. Mike Whitney
12. Basil d'Oliveira — the tour was then cancelled
13. His jaw was broken
14. b) Peter Willey
15. Stan McCabe
16. 45 runs
17. Imran Khan
18. They played Test cricket for two countries
19. John Edrich
20. He became the first overseas batsman to score three Test centuries at Lord's

## 24 · W · WHEN?

1. 1953
2. 1951
3. 1985
4. 1984
5. 1971
6. 1948
7. 1956
8. 1923
9. 1984
10. 1877
11. 1953
12. 1951
13. 1848
14. 1981
15. 1967
16. 1971
17. 1973
18. 1934
19. 1964
20. 1980 — the picture shows Cliff Thorburn

## 25 · C · OLDEST AND YOUNGEST

1. Gary Kasparov
2. Nadia Comaneci
3. Jimmy White
4. Vince Hawkins
5. Leslie Compton
6. Boris Becker
7. b) Gary Player
8. Duncan Edwards
9. Severiano Ballesteros
10. Archie Moore, light-heavyweight champion in 1960
11. Brian Close
12. Paul Allen (West Ham)
13. Mike Tyson
14. Jahangir Khan
15. Wilfred Rhodes
16. Mats Wilander
17. Shooting
18. Mushtaq Mohammad
19. Georges Carpentier
20. Andrea Jaeger

## 26 · BS · AMERICAN STYLE

1. 60 minutes
2. Arnold Palmer — Arnie's Army
3. Basketball
4. Joe diMaggio
5. New England Patriots
6. Bob Tway
7. 1 to 19
8. George Blanda
9. Bob Mathias
10. Boston Celtics
11. Craig Stadler
12. Gerald Ford
13. She lost the America's Cup to Australia
14. George Herman
15. O.J. Simpson — nicknamed 'The Juice'
16. Lee Trevino
17. 1982
18. Walter Camp
19. Lee Elder
20. Bing Crosby (son Nat won)

## 27 · OG · OLYMPIC ODDMENTS

1. Vidal Sassoon
2. Adolf Hitler
3. Ingemar Johansson was disqualified for not trying and forfeited the medal
4. Germany, Italy and Japan
5. John Devitt
6. The Black Power salute (raised clenched fist)
7. He was using an epee wired to register a hit when he hadn't made one
8. He failed a drug test
9. Judo (the Games were in Tokyo)
10. The USSR
11. He was declared a professional sportsman; the medals were restored to his children in 1983
12. The marathon
13. Great Britain
14. Cassius Clay (Muhammad Ali)
15. Shoes
16. 1908
17. USA
18. The Soviet invasion of Afghanistan
19. a) Sailors
20. Alan Wells; he used starting blocks (made compulsory for international competition in 1980)

## 28 · RS · WATER SPORTS

1. David Wilkie
2. Eight
3. *White Crusader*
4. *Morning Cloud*
5. 4½ miles
6. A kayak (as opposed to a canoe)
7. The America's Cup
8. Hammersmith and Barnes
9. Henley Royal Regatta
10. She coxed in the University Boat Race
11. Dawn Fraser
12. A rower has one oar, a sculler two
13. Plymouth
14. Kornelia Ender
15. Canoeing
16. *Superdocious*
17. Its keel
18. Eric Tabarly
19. Buster Crabbe
20. Jack Beresford

## 29 · FE · CONTROVERSIES

1. He scored with his hand
2. Dennis Lillee
3. West Bromwich Albion
4. It was bowled along the ground
5. Martti Vainio
6. Joe Bugner
7. Zola Budd
8. Celtic
9. Douglas Jardine
10. Basketball (1972 Olympic final)
11. Paolo Rossi
12. Antonio Rattin
13. Kevin Moran
14. Tony Greig
15. The Chicago Black Sox
16. Wyndham Halswelle
17. Gene Tunney
18. Newcastle United
19. USA
20. Nikki Pilic

## 30 · W · HOW MANY?

1. Two
2. Seven
3. Four
4. 16
5. None
6. 12. The picture shows Jayne Torvill and Christopher Dean
7. 12
8. Six
9. One
10. 55
11. Three
12. 200
13. 20
14. 28
15. 30
16. Three
17. b) 44
18. 36
19. One — England
20. Nine

## 31 · C · INDOOR SPORTS AND GAMES

1. Kasparov and Karpov
2. Jayne Torvill and Christopher Dean
3. Steve Davis
4. Leighton Rees
5. John Spencer and Ray Reardon
6. The vaulting horse
7. Gillian Gilks
8. Darts
9. Boris Spassky
10. Joe and Fred Davis
11. b) Geoff Hunt
12. Diane and Rosalind Rowe
13. John Lowe
14. Chess
15. Heather Blundell (later Mrs McKay)
16. Joe Johnson; 18 – 12
17. John Campbell
18. Badminton
19. Stefan Lord of Sweden
20. Walter Donaldson

## 32 · BS · RUGBY

1. Phil Bennett, Gareth Edwards, Barbarians v. New Zealand
2. The Kangaroos
3. William Webb Ellis
4. Eddie Waring
5. A fern leaf
6. Dusty Hare
7. It ended in a five-way tie
8. Neil Fox
9. Leeds
10. Mike Campbell-Lamerton
11. Munster
12. J.P.R. Williams
13. Featherstone Rovers
14. Black and white hoops
15. Widnes
16. Dawie de Villiers
17. David Watkins
18. Terry Holmes
19. USA
20. Hull

## 33 · OG · WHEN AND WHERE?

1. Barcelona
2. a) 1948
3. Mexico City
4. 1956
5. Moscow
6. 1896
7. 1980
8. Switzerland
9. Mexico City
10. 1984
11. Paris
12. b) 1936
13. Sarajevo
14. 1952
15. Tokyo
16. 1948, London
17. 1984
18. Helsinki
19. 1976
20. Stockholm

## 35 · FE · THE WORLD CUP

1. The Jules Rimet Trophy
2. Brazil and Italy
3. Jose Luis Brown
4. Uruguay
5. Poland
6. Mexico
7. Just Fontaine
8. Algeria
9. Czechoslovakia
10. Bryan Robson
11. Pickles
12. France, West Germany and Belgium
13. Gerry Armstrong
14. Pele
15. 1958
16. Emilio Butragueno
17. Uwe Seeler
18. Peter Bonetti
19. Graeme Souness
20. 1950 — there was a final pool

## 34 · RS · ANIMALS

1. Longchamp
2. Pigeon racing
3. *Dancing Brave*
4. Five years old
5. *Arkle*, Pat Taaffe
6. Anti-clockwise
7. *Devon Loch*
8. Doncaster
9. Cambridgeshire and Cesarewitch handicaps
10. All of them
11. Coursing
12. Racing pigeons
13. Thoroughbred racehorses
14. Mick the Miller
15. The Curragh
16. It is their 'birthday', i.e. three-year-olds become four-year-olds, etc
17. Blue
18. *L'Escargot*
19. The Kentucky Derby, Belmont Stakes, Preakness Stakes
20. A trotter

## 36 · W · WHICH TROPHY?

1. The Football League Cup
2. The Sheffield Shield
3. The Ryder Cup
4. The Calcutta Cup
5. The Lance Todd Trophy
6. The FA Charity Shield
7. The Full Members' Cup (David Speedie, Chelsea, 1986)
8. The Curtis Cup
9. The Waterloo Handicap
10. The NatWest Trophy
11. The Swaythling Cup
12. The Russell-Cargill Trophy
13. The European Champions Cup
14. The Melbourne Cup
15. The Frank Worrell Trophy
16. The Bowring Bowl
17. The Stanley Cup
18. The Waterloo Cup
19. The Grand Challenge Cup
20. Doggett's Coat and Badge

## 37 · C · MULTIPLE CHAMPIONS

1. Liverpool
2. Jayne Torvill and Christopher Dean
3. Eric Bristow
4. Billie-Jean King
5. c) Gordon Richards
6. C.B. Fry
7. Alain Prost, in 1985 and 1986
8. John Curry
9. Henry Armstrong
10. Surrey
11. Angelo Dundee
12. Lucinda Prior Palmer (later Lucinda Green)
13. Ray Kennedy
14. Wenzel (Andreas and Hanni)
15. *Arkle*
16. Arthur Milton
17. Jim Clark
18. Peter Thomson
19. J.W.H.T. Douglas
20. Maureen Connolly

## 38 · BS · RECORDS

1. Jack Hobbs
2. York City
3. Liverpool, which won the League/Milk Cup for the fourth consecutive time in 1986. The players are Alan Hansen, Kenny Dalglish and Graeme Souness
4. Lee Trevino
5. Pat Jennings
6. Billy Wright
7. Sunil Gavasker
8. Five
9. John McEnroe
10. Joe Payne (10)
11. Mike Gibson
12. Greg Chappell
13. 26–0
14. George Blanda
15. Rod Laver
16. Tich Freeman
17. Dusty Hare
18. Arthur Rowley
19. Nicola Pietrangeli
20. Winston Davis

## 39 · OG · FIELD EVENTS

1. The hop, step and jump
2. Triple jump
3. Long jumper Lynn Davies
4. Bignal
5. The 1500 metres
6. Dick Fosbury, of the 'Fosbury Flop'
7. A gold medal would have been his fourth in the same field event, equalling Al Oerter's record
8. Heide Rosendahl
9. Lynn Davies and Mary Peters
10. The high jump
11. Jurgen Hingsen
12. He lit the flame at the opening ceremony
13. They won the silver medals at every Games
14. Tessa Sanderson and Fatima Whitbread. In 1980 neither qualified for the final
15. a) None
16. Shot put and discus
17. Tug of war
18. Bob Richards
19. It was won by his son, Miklos
20. There is a tower the height of which is exactly the distance of the winning throw: 72·71 metres

## 40 · RS · WHEELS

1. John Surtees
2. The leader in the Tour de France
3. Nigel Mansell
4. Cycling
5. Colin Chapman
6. Belgian
7. Skateboarding
8. Mike Hailwood
9. Graham Hill
10. White-walled tyres
11. Roller skating (International Roller Skating Federation)
12. New Zealander
13. Vanwall
14. Giacomo Agostini
15. Geoff Duke
16. Graham Hill
17. Carlo Ubbiali
18. Roger de Coster
19. George O'Dell
20. Speedway

**41 · FE · TRAGEDY**

1. The Manchester United air crash
2. Ken Barrington
3. Maureen Connolly
4. Lima, Peru
5. The Fastnet race
6. Ewen Chatfield
7. *Dawn Run*
8. Bert Trautmann
9. Jock Stein
10. Graham Hill
11. Johnny Owen
12. Lillian Board
13. Jack Lovelock
14. Ibrox Park
15. John White
16. Rocky Marciano
17. Derek Dooley
18. J.W.H.T. Douglas
19. Stanley Ketchel
20. Mike Hawthorn and Donald Campbell

**43 · C · FAMOUS WORDS AND FACES**

1. Muhammad Ali
2. Diego Maradona, against England in the World Cup, 1986
3. Terry Venables
4. John McEnroe
5. Frank Bruno
6. Bill Shankly
7. C. Old = Chilly (cold)
8. Ian Botham
9. Douglas Jardine, swatting a fly during the bodyline series
10. Barry McGuigan
11. His nose. His nickname is 'Bignose'
12. Bobby Robson
13. Sussex (David Sheppard)
14. Grandfather
15. Ramadhin and Valentine
16. Ron Atkinson
17. Tony Sibson and Marvin Hagler
18. Geoff Boycott
19. Lester Piggott, after his record 28th Classic victory
20. Dennis Lillee

**42 · W · WHICH TEAM?**

1. The England World Cup Squad
2. Yorkshire
3. The Washington Redskins
4. New York Cosmos
5. c) Surrey
6. Chelsea
7. John Hurt, who played Bob Champion (on *Aldaniti*)
8. Chicago Bears
9. Cardiff City
10. India
11. Leeds United
12. Leicester
13. Shrewsbury Town
14. Cincinnati Bengals
15. Real Madrid
16. Houston Oilers
17. China
18. Everton
19. Collegers and Oppidans
20. The New York Mets

**44 · BS · STICK AND BALL**

1. Payne Stewart
2. Australia
3. Cricket umpires
4. Barry Hearn
5. Polo
6. Golf
7. 4½in (10·8cm)
8. Hockey
9. Jose-Maria Olazabal
10. Billiards
11. 22
12. Baseball
13. Somerset, Sussex and Northants
14. Augusta
15. Hurling
16. Croquet
17. Seven points
18. Twelve
19. Golf
20. Cricket — he was a famous Surrey player

## 45 · OG · WINTER OLYMPICS

1. Maurice Ravel
2. Canada
3. John Curry and Robin Cousins
4. Eric Heiden
5. Sonja Henie
6. Ingemar Stenmark
7. Shooting and skiing
8. East Germany
9. St Moritz
10. Bill Johnson
11. Jean-Claude Killy
12. Mahre
13. Goitschel
14. Two
15. Salchow
16. 2-man bobsleigh
17. Leonhard Stock
18. The Nordic skiing 50km cross-country
19. The ski jumps
20. Jeanette Altwegg (1952)

## 46 · RS · THE GRAND NATIONAL

1. *West Tip*
2. *Red Rum*
3. Aintree
4. Mrs Jenny Pitman
5. *Crisp*, Richard Pitman
6. Bob Champion
7. The Melling Road
8. 30
9. Fred Winter
10. Lord Oaksey (John Lawrence)
11. Captain Becher — the famous fence has been Becher's Brook to this day
12. Red: *Red Rum* and *Red Alligator*
13. Fred Rimell
14. *Golden Miller*
15. Noel le Mare
16. There was a pile-up at the 23rd fence involving the whole field but the winner
17. 66
18. *Arkle* never ran in the Grand National
19. Pierre 'Teazy-Weazy' Raymond
20. *Russian Hero*

## 47 · FE · IT'S A RECORD

1. Pat Jennings
2. Jimmy Greaves
3. David Moorcroft
4. Martina Navratilova
5. b) Glenn Turner
6. Kenny Dalglish
7. Geoffrey Boycott
8. Gunder Hägg
9. Sunderland
10. Hanif Mohammad
11. Jimmy McGrory
12. Bobby Fischer
13. Jess Willard
14. Emil Zatopek, Gordon Pirie, Derek Ibbotson and Chris Chataway
15. Sunil Gavasker
16. 36–0 (Arbroath v. Bon Accord)
17. Laszlo Papp
18. Alf Common
19. Suzanne Lenglen
20. Renton and Celtic

## 48 · W · WHICH VENUE?

1. a) Ascot
2. The Guild Hall, Preston
3. Le Mans
4. Tokyo
5. Henley
6. Cheltenham
7. The National Exhibition Centre, Birmingham
8. City Ground and Meadow Lane, Nottingham (Forest and County)
9. The St Lawrence Ground
10. Bernabeu Stadium, Madrid
11. Royal Lytham and St Anne's
12. Craven Cottage, Fulham
13. The Bislett Stadium
14. Hampden Park, Glasgow
15. England
16. Madison Square Gardens
17. Stade Roland Garros
18. Cap Gris Nez
19. Candlestick Park
20. Eden Park, Auckland and Eden Gardens, Calcutta

## 49 · C · NICKNAMES

1. Barry McGuigan
2. Greg Norman and Jack Nicklaus
3. Muhammad Ali (or Cassius Clay)
4. The Crafty Cockney
5. John McEnroe
6. Snooker players Alex Higgins and Jimmy White
7. Lynn Davies
8. Ken Rosewall
9. West Bromwich Albion
10. Pele
11. Gilbert Jessop
12. Jimmy Wilde, flyweight champion
13. Alberto Juantorena
14. Nat Lofthouse
15. Derek Randall
16. Harry Greb, middleweight champion
17. Gertrude Moran
18. Primo Carnera, the 'Ambling Alp'
19. Harry Wragg
20. Len Shackleton

## 50 · BS · FOOTBALL VARIATIONS

1. Australian rules football
2. 60–0
3. Southampton
4. Derby County
5. Barcelona and Napoli
6. American football
7. Max Boyce
8. Jimmy Greaves
9. France
10. Warrington
11. American football
12. b) The Wallabies
13. Dave McKay
14. Keith Fielding
15. Llanelli rugby union side
16. Gaelic football
17. The Pontypool front row
18. Canadian football
19. Partick Thistle
20. Vince Lombardi

## 51 · OG · RECORD BREAKERS

1. Gymnast Nadia Comaneci
2. Mark Spitz
3. Bob Beamon
4. Mary Peters
5. Johnny Weissmuller
6. Eight
7. Lasse Viren
8. Alberto Juantorena
9. Herb Elliott
10. Canada
11. David Wilkie
12. Shooting
13. The men's 4x100 metres relay
14. Vladimir Salnikov
15. Miruts Yifter
16. Vasili Alexeev
17. Jesse Owens
18. Larissa Latynina
19. Michael Gross
20. Carl Lewis, Jesse Owens: 100 metres, 200 metres, 4x100 metres relay, long jump

## 52 · RS · RACING MISCELLANY

1. Bruno Malinowski
2. Four: freestyle, butterfly, breaststroke, backstroke
3. Edinburgh
4. It hit a moored tug
5. Steve Jones
6. Jim Clark and Jackie Stewart
7. Cycling
8. Tommy Stack
9. Kip Keino
10. Downhill, slalom, giant slalom
11. *Liberty*
12. Trap six
13. Francis Chichester
14. Murray Halberg
15. *Dancing Brave*
16. The former are downhill, the latter cross-country
17. Yachting
18. Motor racing
19. Charlotte Brew
20. b) Stan Mellor

## 53 · FE · IN THE RING

1. J.B. Williamson
2. Tim Witherspoon
3. a) Kinshasa, Zaire
4. British heavyweight title
5. John Mugabi
6. Archie Moore
7. Queens Park Rangers
8. Light-heavyweight
9. Duke McKenzie
10. Rocky Graziano
11. The 26th
12. Floyd Patterson
13. Patrizio Oliva
14. They retired undefeated as heavyweight champions, and did not make a comeback
15. Chris Finnegan (Olympic title)
16. Roberto Duran
17. Ken Buchanan
18. He failed to make the weight for a title fight
19. Max and Buddy Baer
20. Jack and Brian London

## 54 · W · WHICH SPORT?

1. Baseball
2. Ice-hockey
3. Weightlifting
4. American football
5. Soccer
6. Bowls — the picture shows W.G. Grace
7. Darts
8. Trampolining
9. Figure skating
10. Baseball
11. Fencing
12. Angling
13. Skiing
14. Yachting — the America's Cup
15. Basketball
16. Curling
17. Horse racing — all Grand National winners
18. Hockey
19. Wrestling
20. Judo

Photographic Acknowledgements
Photographs courtesy of Syndication International

Picture research by Sheila Corr